BUCKEYE HERITAGE

OHIO'S HISTORY IN SONG

by Elizabeth Anne Salt

ENTHEA PRESS
COLUMBUS, OHIO — ATLANTA, GEORGIA

ISBN: 0-89804-813-3

Publisher's Cataloging-In-Publication Data

Salt, Elizabeth Anne.
    Buckeye Heritage: Ohio's history in song / by Elizabeth Anne Salt.
    p.   cm.
    Includes bibliographical references (p.   )
    ISBN 0-89804-813-3
    1. Folk songs, American—Ohio. 2. Ballads, American—Ohio. 3. Ohio—Songs and music. 4. Ohio—History. I. Title.
M1629.7.037
782.421'62

Table of Songs

To all Ohioans,
past, present, and future

ACKNOWLEDGEMENTS

I would like to thank the people who have inspired me and helped me in the development of this book. Jacqueline Wallace was kind enough to translate the lyrics of the two French voyageur songs. Using her translations, I was able to create English interpretations which are true to the meaning of the songs and also can be sung to the traditional French Canadian tunes. My sister-in-law, Janet Salt, was very helpful and patient in checking and correcting my song arrangements and made many useful suggestions for improving them.

Numerous folk musician friends have given me guidance — in particular I would like to thank Steven K. Smith, Marji Hazen, and Sylvia Miller. I am also grateful to Lorraine Lee Hammond, Sally Rogers, and Madeline MacNeil for the inspiring examples they have been to me.

Carl Japikse was very helpful in preparing the manuscript and publishing it as a finished book.

My parents, Charles and Alice Salt, have my sincere gratitude for standing behind me throughout this project and for constantly encouraging me to pursue my inspiration.

PREFACE

   Buckeye Heritage: Ohio's History In Song is a presentation of the rich history of the state through traditional songs that have been written and sung about events that have shaped Ohio's destiny. A brief sketch of the historical context of each song is presented as an introduction to the song. These sketches are not intended to provide comprehensive accounts of the history of each event that is covered but, rather, are included to give general background information so that the historical basis of each song can be understood and appreciated. If more in-depth information about particular aspects of Ohio's history is needed, an extensive bibliography of sources is provided at the back of the song book.

   Some of the songs included in this book are traditional, while others have known authors, but all derive from the nineteenth century or earlier. All of the songs are in the public domain to the best of my knowledge.

   Song arrangements have intentionally been kept simple, so that people with a minimum of musical expertise can enjoy them. Those with greater musical backgrounds can create more complex arrangements of these tunes to fit their skills. Many of the songs have been arranged in the key of D to facilitate playing them on the mountain dulcimer, which is normally played in that key. Dulcimer tablature has been included in an appendix for all songs that can be played on the diatonic fretboard of the dulcimer. On songs for which a capo is needed, the dulcimer fret numbers are counted from the nut rather than from the capo, but the capoed fret is considered the open or zero fret.

   Most songs in other keys which are included can be played on the dulcimer using chords.

   On some songs with many verses, only selected verses have been included. On many of the ballads, it has been necessary to include all the verses so that the context of the story told by the song is not lost or confused.

I hope that these songs will provide pleasure and enjoyment to those who sing them as well as serving as a means of broadening appreciation for the rich heritage we have inherited as citizens of the state of Ohio.

Elizabeth Salt
June 1992

BUCKEYE HERITAGE

OHIO'S HISTORY IN SONG

The earliest evidence of Indian settlement in Ohio dates from about 15,000 years ago. Ohio's first prehistoric Indians were primarily nomadic or seasonally nomadic hunters and gatherers. Much later, a more sedentary lifestyle developed with the advent of agriculture in Ohio around 1500 B.C. Two mound building traditions arose after agricultural subsistence and sedentary settlement patterns were established. The first of these, the Adena tradition, began to develop about 1000 B.C. and flourished until around 100 A.D. The Adena people built villages of circular wooden dwellings and buried their dead in log tombs within conical earthen mounds. Some effigy mounds, such as the Serpent Mound in Adams County, were also constructed during the Adena period. Their purpose remains unknown. The Adena were the first Indians in Ohio to practice extensive agriculture. They raised pumpkins, squash, beans, and sunflowers and were also the first pottery makers in Ohio. They made unpainted grit-tempered ceramics.

The Hopewell people, who lived in Ohio from about 100 B.C. to 800 A.D., were also Mound Builders. They constructed clusters of burial mounds surrounded by geometric earthworks. They were the first group in Ohio to cultivate corn. The Hopewell people had extensive trade networks with other Indian groups and obtained many items not found in Ohio, including mica (from the Carolinas), obsidian (from Wyoming), and copper (from the Lake Superior area). Archaeologists are not sure what caused the decline of the Mound Builders.

The Fort Ancient (southern Ohio) and Whittlesey Focus people (northeastern Ohio) lived in Ohio from about 800 A.D. to 1600 A.D. They practiced intensive agriculture and built fortified villages of rectangular wattle and daub dwellings with thatched roofs. They buried

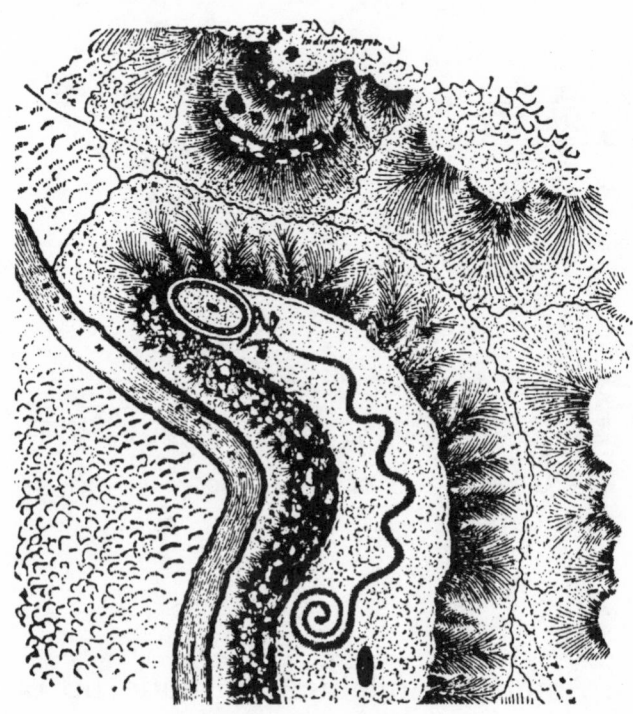

SERPENT MOUND

their dead in pits in the ground. It is thought that these people were either annihilated or driven west of Ohio by Iroquois raids during the 1600's.

The Iroquois used Ohio as a hunting ground during the 1600's, but few other Indians lived in the area during the seventeenth century. Early in the eighteenth century, after Iroquois control of the Ohio Valley weakened, various other Indian groups began to migrate into Ohio and settle there. These included people from the Shawnee, Miami, Wyandot, Ottawa, Chippewa, and Delaware tribes. The name Mingo is given to Iroquois who remained and settled in Ohio during this time.

"Iroquois Lullaby" is a traditional lullaby sung by Iroquois women to calm and soothe their babies. "Farewell to the Warriors" is a traditional Chippewa song sung by the women as the men departed for battle.

IROQUOIS LULLABY

Traditional

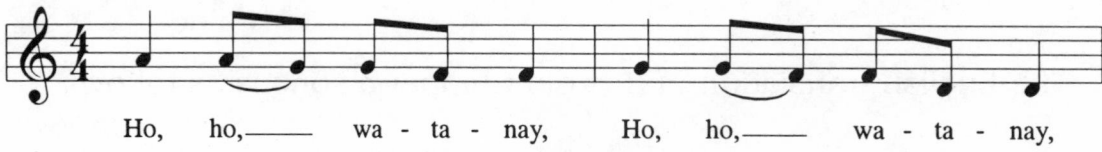

Ho, ho,—— wa - ta - nay, Ho, ho,—— wa - ta - nay,

Ho, ho,—— wa - ta - nay, Ki - yo - ke - na, Ki - yo - ke - na.

This song, like many Native American lullabies, is made up of meaningless syllables which are repeated over and over again.

FAREWELL TO THE WARRIORS

Traditional

Um - be, A - ni - ma - djag, Wa - su -

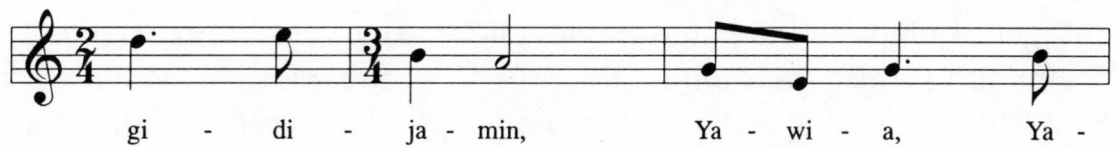

gi - di - ja - min, Ya - wi - a, Ya -

wi - a, Ya, Ya - wi - a, Ya - wi - a - a - a.

The English translation of this old Chippewa song is as follows:

Um be....................... Come.
A ni ma djag............... It is time for you to depart.
Wa su gi di ja min ...... We are going on a long journey.
Ya wi a .... (Meaningless syllables)

This song was traditionally sung as a war party was leaving a Chippewa village.

The French were the first Europeans to set foot in Ohio. Louis Joliet, a French explorer and fur trader, discovered Lake Erie in 1669. René Robert Cavelier, Sieur de La Salle is thought to have made an exploratory expedition through Ohio in 1669 and 1670, although little historical evidence remains of it. French coureur-de-bois (fur traders) probably were active in Ohio during the early eighteenth century, and voyageurs taking furs from the Great Lakes to Montreal undoubtedly passed through Lake Erie at this time.

English traders from Pennsylvania, Virginia, and the Carolinas also reached Ohio during the eighteenth century. By the 1740's, English traders predominated in Ohio, rather than French, and both England and France claimed the Ohio country. The French sought to restore their influence among the Ohio Indians by sending Céloron de Bienville on an expedition through the Ohio region in 1749. He buried a number of lead plates, claiming the territory for France, along major rivers throughout the area. He traveled into Lake Erie, through Lake Chatauqua, and down the Allegheny River to the Ohio River. He then journeyed down the Ohio to the mouth of the Great Miami River and from there traveled overland to Pickawillany, a large Miami Indian village in western Ohio (near present-day Piqua). From there he went north to the Maumee River and back into Lake Erie. Two of the six plates he buried were later found—one in 1798 at the mouth of the Muskingum River and one in 1846 at the mouth of the Kanawha River. Céloron de Bienville's expedition had no significant impact on the Indians of the Ohio country, and they continued to develop stronger trade ties with the English than with the French throughout the mid-1700's.

The French voyageurs and explorers, however, have left a colorful legacy of song. "C'est l'Aviron Qui Nous Mene En Haut" is a traditional voyageur canoe paddling song. The title translates into English as "It Is The Oar That Impels Us On."

"Petit Rocher De La Haute Montagne" is a voyageur lament. It is based upon an historical incident in which a voyageur named Cadieux became lost in the forest and died after his party of traders was attacked by the Iroquois. The actual incident took place in Canada, but the song that was later sung about it was well known in all areas where French voyageurs traveled.

C'EST L'AVIRON QUI NOUS MENE EN HAUT
(ENGLISH WORDS)

Traditional

On my re - turn from beau - ti - ful Ro - chel - le,

On my re - turn from beau - ti - ful Ro - chel - le,

There I did meet three pret - ty and fair mai - dens.

CHORUS:

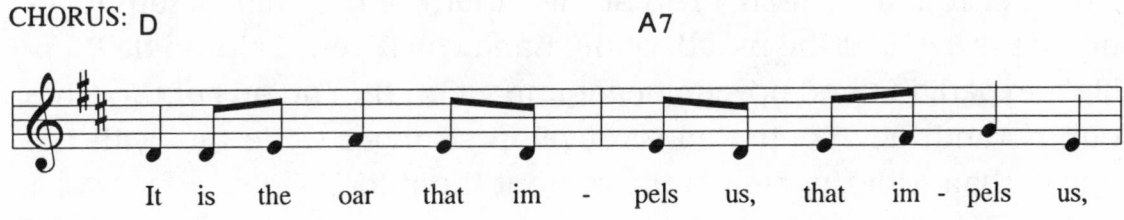

It is the oar that im - pels us, that im - pels us,

It is the oar that im - pels us on.

There I did meet three pretty and fair maidens,
There I did meet three pretty and fair maidens,
I did not choose but took the one most lovely.
Chorus

I did not choose but took the one most lovely,
I did not choose but took the one most lovely,
I put her up behind me on my saddle.
Chorus

I put her up behind me on my saddle,
I put her up behind me on my saddle,
A hundred leagues I rode without speaking.
Chorus

French words:

M'en revenant de la jolie Rochelle,
M'en revenant de la jolie Rochelle,
J'ai rencontré trois jolies demoiselles.

Chorus:
C'est l'aviron qui nous mene, qui nous mene,
C'est l'aviron qui nous mene en haut.

J'ai rencontré trois jolies demoiselles,
J'ai rencontré trois jolies demoiselles,
J'ai point choisi, mais j'ai pris la plus belle.
Chorus

J'ai point choisi, mais j'ai pris la plus belle,
J'ai point choisi, mais j'ai pris la plus belle,
Je l'y fis monter derrière moi, sur ma selle.
Chorus

Je l'y fis monter derrière moi, sur ma selle,
Je l'y fis monter derrière moi, sur ma selle,
J'y fis cent lieues sans parler avec elle.
Chorus

PETIT ROCHER DE LA HAUTE MONTAGNE
(ENGLISH WORDS)

Traditional

Oh, lit - tle rock up - on the high moun - tain peak,

Here I have come to end this life, new trails to seek.

Ah, sweet e - choes, oh, hear my sigh - ing breath,

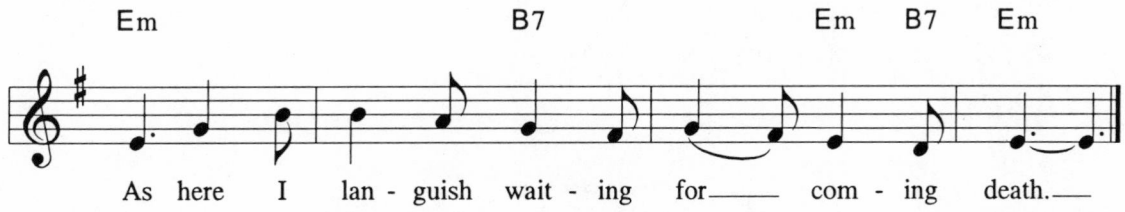

As here I lan - guish wait - ing for com - ing death.

Oh, little birds your soft and gentle harmony,
When you do sing, you bring life back again to me.
Ah, if I had wings to fly like you do,
I would be happy when two days were through.

My knees do bend, my feeble voice grows weak and still,
I fall, alas, and prepare to depart I will.
I am alone, no one to comfort me,
When cold death comes, how desolate can I be.

18

It is then here that the world abandons me,
  But I have you, Savior of humanity!
Blessed Virgin, be with me where I lie,
  Hold me in your loving arms as I die.

French words:

Petit rocher de la haute montagne,
  Je viens ici finir cette campagne.
Ah! doux échos, entendez mes soupirs.
  En languissant, je vais bientôt mourir.

Petits oiseaux, vos douces harmonies,
  Quand vous chantez, me rattachent à la vie.
Ah! si j'avais des ailes comme vous,
  Je serais heureux avant qu'il fût deux jours!

Mes genoux plient; ma faible voix s'arrête.
  Je tombe...Hélas! à partir ils s'apprêtent.
Je reste seul...Pas un qui me console,
  Quant la mort vient par un si grand désole!

C'est donc ici que le monde m'abandonne!
  Mais j'ai recours en vous, Sauveur des hommes!
Très Sainte Vierge, ne m'abandonnez pas.
  Permettez-moi de mourir entre vos bras!

In the spring of 1774, tensions between the Ohio Indians and the English frontiersmen were growing as the result of isolated acts of violence on both sides. Increasing numbers of hunters, traders and surveyors were entering the Ohio country from Pennsylvania and Virginia. Some were honest men, and some were scoundrels. One of the worst atrocities that occurred during that spring was the unprovoked murder of a group of Mingo Indians at a place called "Baker's Cabin" (near present-day Steubenville, Ohio). The Indians were given whiskey, and when they had become drunk, they were killed by a party of marauding frontiersmen, led by Jacob Greathouse. Among those killed were several members of the family of the Mingo chief, Logan.

Logan, who had heretofore been friendly to white settlers, sought vengeance and killed many people living on the Pennsylvania frontier during the summer of 1774. Later, in the fall of that year, Logan refused to attend peace negotiations to end Lord Dunmore's War. Instead, he delivered a speech to a representative of the Virginia Militia who had gone to his village to speak with him. Logan's speech has become a famous example of Indian oratory. He stated:

> I appeal to any white man to say, if ever he entered Logan's cabin hungry and he gave him not meat; if ever he came cold and naked and he clothed him not. During the course of the last, long and bloody war, Logan remained idle in his cabin, an advocate for peace. Such was my love for the whites that my countrymen pointed as they passed and said, "Logan is a friend of white men." I had even thought to live with you but for the injuries of one man. Colonel Cresap the last spring in cold blood and unprovoked murdered all the relatives of Logan; not sparing even his women and children. There runs not a drop of my blood in the veins of any living creature. This called upon me for revenge. I have sought it. I have killed many. I have fully glutted my vengeance. For my country, I rejoice at the beams of peace. Yet do not harbor the thought that mine is the joy of fear. Logan never felt fear. He will not turn on his heel to save his life. Who is there to mourn for Logan? Not one.

Chief Logan laid the blame on Michael Cresap, the leader of a

Pennsylvania frontier militia, but it was later discovered that Jacob Greathouse was responsible for the ruthless massacre. Tradition states that Logan's speech was delivered in the shade of a large elm tree. Although the tree died in 1965, one can still visit Logan Elm State Memorial in southern Pickaway County and see several monuments to Chief Logan and other historic Ohio Indians.

The song "Logan's Lament" presents a rather romanticized version of the story of the murder of Chief Logan's family and of his vengeance and remorse. Its authorship is unknown, but it was probably written during the early nineteenth century.

THE LOGAN ELM, 1876

LOGAN'S LAMENT

Traditional

The black - bird is sing - ing on Mich - i - gan's

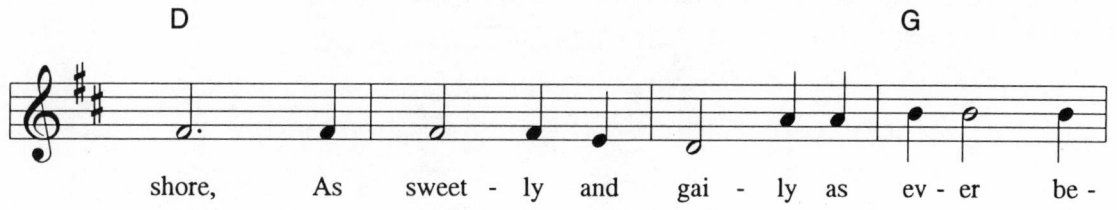

shore, As sweet - ly and gai - ly as ev - er be -

fore. For she knows to her mate she at plea - sure can

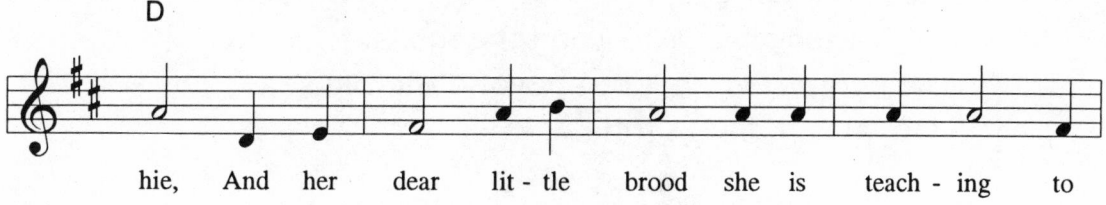

hie, And her dear lit - tle brood she is teach - ing to

fly. Oh, a - las, I am un - done.

Each bird and each beast are as blessed in degree.
All nature is cheerful; all happy but me.
I will go to my tent and lie down in despair.
I will paint me with black, and I'll sever my hair.
      Oh, alas, I am undone.

I will sit on the shore where the hurricane blows,
And reveal to the god of the tempest my woes.
I will weep for a season on bitterness fed,
For my kindred have gone to the hills of the dead.
      Oh, alas, I am undone.

But they died not of hunger or lingering decay.
The steel of the white man has swept them away.
The snake skin that once I so sacredly wore
I will toss with disdain to the storm-beaten shore.
      Oh, alas, I am undone.

They came to my cabin when heaven was black.
I heard not their coming, and I knew not their track.
But I saw by the light of their flaming fusils,
They were people engendered beyond the big sea.
      Oh, alas, I am undone.

I will dig up my hatchet and bend my old bow.
By night and by day, I will follow the foe.
No lake shall impede me, nor mountains nor snow.
For their blood alone can give my spirit repose.
      Oh, alas, I am undone.

My wife and my children; oh spare me the tale.
For who is there left that is kin to Gee-hail.
My wife and my children; oh spare me the tale.
For who is there left that is kin to Gee-hail.
      Oh, alas I am undone.

The murder of Chief Logan's family and the resulting repercussions were important catalysts of Lord Dunmore's War. John Murray, Earl of Dunmore, the governor of Virginia, organized a militia to combat marauding Indians in June, 1774.

A large part of Lord Dunmore's force, under Colonel Andrew Lewis, was attacked at the confluence of the Ohio and Kanawha Rivers by over a thousand Indians on October 10, 1774. An all day battle ensued and ended only when the Indians retreated back to the north side of the Ohio River at dusk. The Virginians considered themselves victorious, although one-fifth of their number had been killed or wounded, since the Indians withdrew in the end. The battle became known as the Battle of Point Pleasant. Following the battle, Lord Dunmore's army marched north into the Ohio country and established a camp in what is now Pickaway County. Here, peace negotiations took place, and it was agreed that the Indians would turn over all white prisoners to Lord Dunmore and would regard the Ohio River as the southern boundary of their territory. The most important outcome of Lord Dunmore's War and its single battle is the fact that it paved the way for the settlement of Kentucky, since the terms of the treaty forbade the Indians to build villages south of the Ohio River.

LORD DUNMORE

A small museum and a monument to the Battle of Point Pleasant can be found in Point Pleasant, West Virginia, today. The song "The Battle of Point Pleasant" takes the form of a traditional ballad, which tells a story and recounts the major events of the battle.

BATTLE OF POINT PLEASANT

Traditional

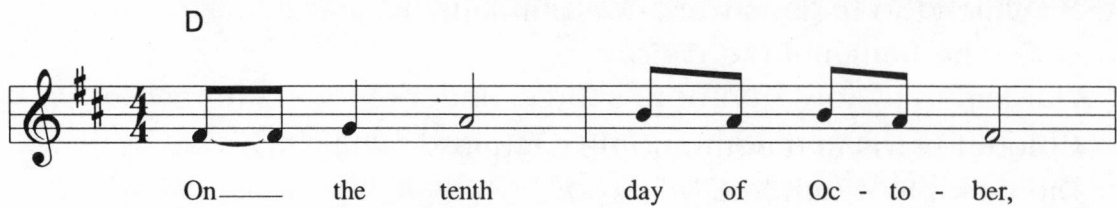

On the tenth day of Oc - to - ber,

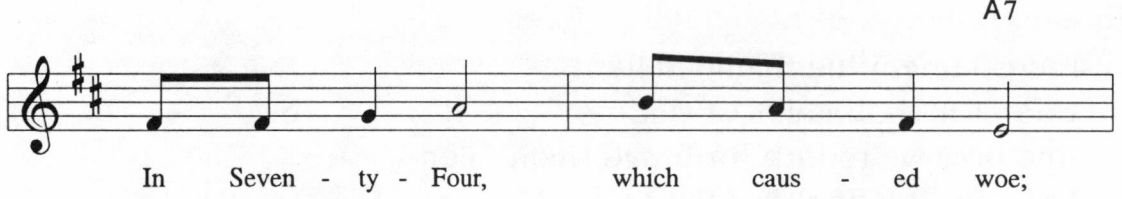

In Seven - ty - Four, which caus - ed woe;

The In - dian war - ri - ors did cov - er,

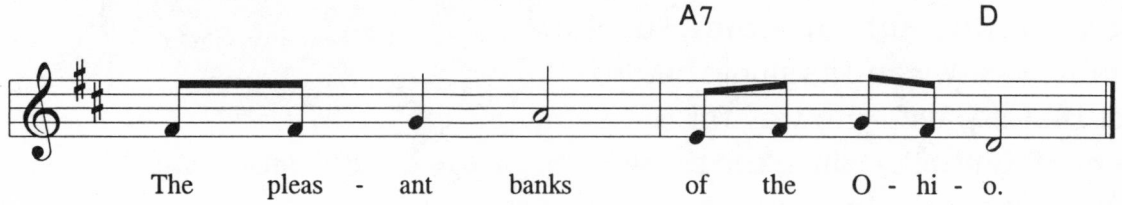

The pleas - ant banks of the O - hi - o.

Judgment proceeds to execution —
Let fame throughout all dangers go;
Our heroes fought with resolution
Upon the banks of the Ohio.

The battle beginning in the morning —
Throughout the day it lasted so,
Till evening shadows were returning
Upon the banks of the Ohio.

Seven score lay dead and wounded,
Of champions that faced the foe;
By which the Indians were confounded
Upon the banks of the Ohio.

Colonel Lewis and some noble captains,
Did down to death like Uriah go;
Alas, their heads wound up in napkins
Upon the banks of the Ohio.

Kings lament the mighty fallen
Upon the mountains of Gilboa;
And now we mourn for brave Hugh Allen
Far from the banks of the Ohio.

Oh, bless the mighty King of Heaven,
For all his wondrous works below,
Who hath to us the victory given
Upon the banks of the Ohio.

In 1772, a group of Moravians (a German Protestant sect) established a mission among the Delaware Indians in eastern Ohio. Their first settlement was located on the Tuscarawas River and was called Schoenbrunn. Several Moravian families, under the leadership of David Zeisberger and John Heckewelder, worked with converted Delaware Indians and taught them Christian virtues and Moravian concepts of pacifism.

By 1780, three Moravian Delaware villages existed in close proximity to each other — Schoenbrunn, Salem, and Gnadenhutten. The Moravian Indians sought to remain neutral during the Revolutionary War, and supporters of both the British and the American causes received friendly treatment in the Moravian towns. However, this attitude caused the military on both sides to suspect that the Moravians were aiding the enemy. In the fall of 1781, some British rangers and their Indian allies plundered the Moravian towns and forced the Moravian Indians to move farther west, to the region of Upper Sandusky, for the winter. In February, 1782, the Moravian Indians, who were by then facing starvation, were permitted to send one hundred fifty people back to their Tuscarawas River towns to harvest the corn left in the fields during their forced departure the previous fall.

While they were harvesting the corn, the Indians at Gnadenhutten and Salem were discovered by a volunteer militia of frontiersmen from Pennsylvania led by Colonel David Williamson. The militia, incensed by recent Indian raids (in which the Moravian Indians had taken no part), decided to take their vengeance on these people. The Moravian Indians were disarmed and imprisoned in two cabins at Gnadenhutten. The next morning they were led out of the cabins in pairs and were murdered. Sixty-two adults and thirty-four children were killed in the Gnadenhutten massacre. Two young boys escaped as the massacre was occurring. They were able to warn the Indians at Schoenbrunn, who fled before the militia arrived there.

The song "Jesus, Hear Our Prayer" is an early Moravian hymn. It may have been sung in the Moravian settlements of eastern Ohio.

JESUS, HEAR OUR PRAYER

Count Nicholas L. Zinzendorf

Adam Drese

The Ordinance of 1787 created the Northwest Territory (which would later become the states of Ohio, Indiana, Illinois, Michigan, and Wisconsin), and General Arthur St. Clair became the first territorial governor of the Northwest Territory. The first permanent settlement in Ohio was founded at Marietta in 1788. However, the westward expansion of American settlement following the Revolutionary War caused renewed friction with the Indians of Ohio.

In 1790, the militias of Kentucky, Virginia, and western Pennsylvania were called to gather at Fort Washington (Cincinnati) to prepare to subdue the Indians. This force of 1400 to 1500 men was led by General Josiah Harmar. The militia was poorly trained and, though they destroyed several Indian villages, they were eventually repulsed by the Indians and forced to retreat to Cincinnati.

In September, 1791, General Arthur St. Clair led another militia north through western Ohio, where they sought to establish a series of forts. This army was attacked by a large force of Indians as they camped on the east fork of the Wabash River (at the site of present-day Fort Recovery, Ohio) on November 4, 1791. The militia was disorganized and suffered tremendous losses. Over 900 militiamen were killed or seriously wounded, while only about sixty Indians were killed. This battle, known as St. Clair's Defeat, was the Ohio Indians' biggest victory and one of the United States military's worst defeats.

ARTHUR ST. CLAIR

In the spring of 1793, a new frontier army, under the command of General Anthony Wayne was organized at Cincinnati. The army was carefully prepared and drilled throughout the summer and began to march northward in October of 1793. They established winter quarters at Fort Greene Ville (present-day Greenville, Ohio) and also built a fort at the site of St. Clair's defeat, which was appropriately called Fort Recovery. In June of 1794, an unsuccessful attack was made on Fort Recovery by the Indians. During the summer of that year, Anthony Wayne's army advanced farther north building an additional fort, named Fort Defiance, at the confluence of the Auglaize and Maumee Rivers. This well-trained

army engaged a mixed group of Shawnee and Miami Indians in battle at Fallen Timbers (so named because a tornado had toppled many large trees there) on August 20, 1794. In less than an hour, the Indian attack was repulsed, and the Indians were fleeing the battleground.

As a result of the defeat they suffered at Fallen Timbers, the Indians met with Anthony Wayne at Fort Greene Ville from June to August of 1795, and a peace treaty was concluded. The Treaty of Greenville established new boundaries between Indian and American territory. The Indians were permitted to continue to live in the northwestern quarter of Ohio, but the remainder of the territory was surrendered to the United States.

The song "St. Clair's Defeat" is a ballad which tells the story of this major battle of the Ohio Indian Wars. A small museum, a reconstructed fortress, and a monument commemorating both battles which occurred there can be visited in Fort Recovery, Ohio.

ST. CLAIR'S DEFEAT

At Bunker's Hill and Quebec, where many a hero fell,
Likewise at Long Island, it is I the truth can tell.
But such a dreadful carnage may I never see again
As happened near St. Mary's upon the river plain.

Our army was attack-ed just as the day did dawn,
And soon was overpower-ed and driven from the lawn.
They killed Major Oldham, Lemon, and Briggs likewise,
While fierce yells of Indians resounded through the skies.

They had not been long broken when General Butler found
Himself so badly wounded he was forced to quit the ground.
"My God!" says he, "what shall we do; we're wounded every man.
Go charge them, valiant heroes, and beat them if you can."

We charged again with courage firm, but soon again gave ground.
The war whoop was redoubled, as were the foes around.
They killed Major Ferguson, which caused his men to cry,
"Our only safety is in flight or fighting here to die!"

Yet three hours more we fought them, 'till at last we had to yield,
When nine hundred bloody warriors lay stretched upon the field.
Said Colonel Gibson to his men, "My boys, be not dismayed,
I am sure that true Virginians were never yet afraid."

"Ten thousand deaths I'd rather die than they should gain the field."
With that he got the fatal shot that caus-ed him to yield.
Said Major Clark, "My heroes, we can here no longer stand.
We'll strive to form an order and retreat the best we can."

The word "Retreat!" being passed around there was a dismal cry.
Then helter-skelter through the woods like wolves and sheep they fly!
This well-appointed army, which but a day before
Had brave defied all danger was like a cloud passed o'er.

Alas, the dying and wounded, how dreadful was the thought!
To the tomahawk and scalping knife in misery are brought.
Some had a thigh and some an arm broke on the field that day,
Who writhed in torment at the stake to close the dire affray.

To mention our brave officers is what I wish to do.
No sons of Mars fought e'er so brave or with such courage true.
To Captain Bradford I belonged; to his artillery,
He fell that day amongst the slain, a valiant man was he.

The signing of the Treaty of Greenville in August, 1795 paved the way for a rapid growth in the pioneer settlement of Ohio, since the Indians no longer posed a threat to farms and villages. People moving into Ohio at that time generally acquired their land for settlement in one of three ways — either from the United States Land Office, from a previous owner, or from a private land company. As people settled their newly purchased tracts of land, the task they faced was formidable. They had to clear the forest from the land before they could begin to plant their first crops; then cabins had to be built using the timber which had been cut.

Most of Ohio's early pioneers settled along the rivers, which provided the main means of transportation in a wilderness which as yet had few roads. In spite of the hardships, settlers flocked to Ohio. So many people came so quickly that Governor St. Clair found it necessary to take a census in 1797. It was discovered that just over 5000 free adult males resided in Ohio at that time. Since this was the number needed for the formation of a territorial legislature, elections were held in December, 1798 to choose twenty-two members for the lower house of the legislature.

"Pleasant Ohio" is a song from the settlement era extolling the beauty and abundance of Ohio and providing encouragement for Easterners to "move out west" and settle in Ohio. The song became widely known all over the Midwest during the pioneer era, and numerous variations developed under such titles as "Lovely Ohio" and "Shoot the Buffalo."

PLEASANT OHIO

Traditional

Come ___ all ye fine young fel -

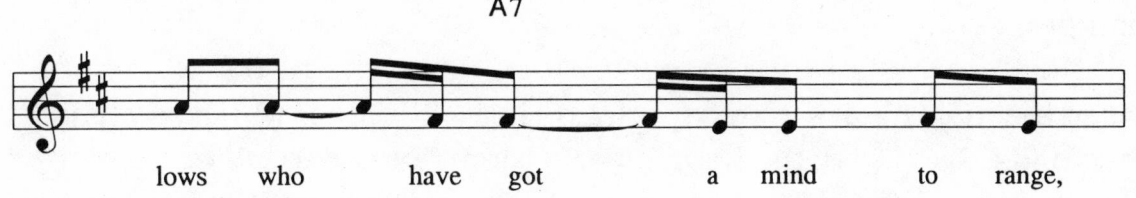

lows who have got a mind to range,

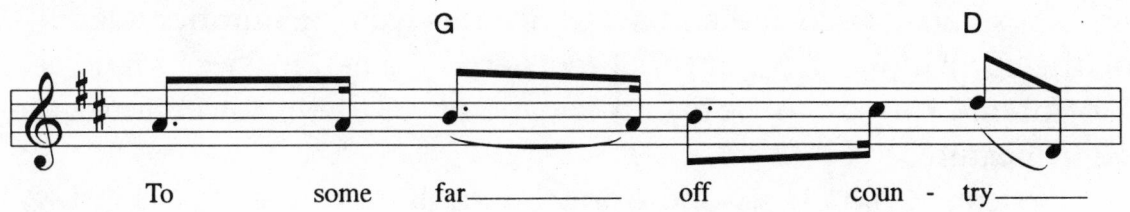

To some far ___ off coun - try ___

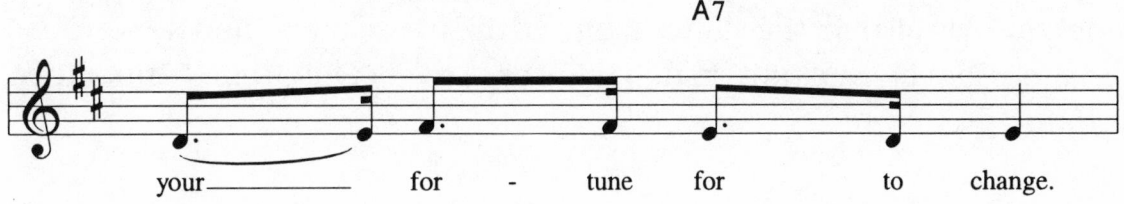

your ___ for - tune for to change.

We'll ___ set - tle in the land

of ___ the plea - sant O - hi - o;

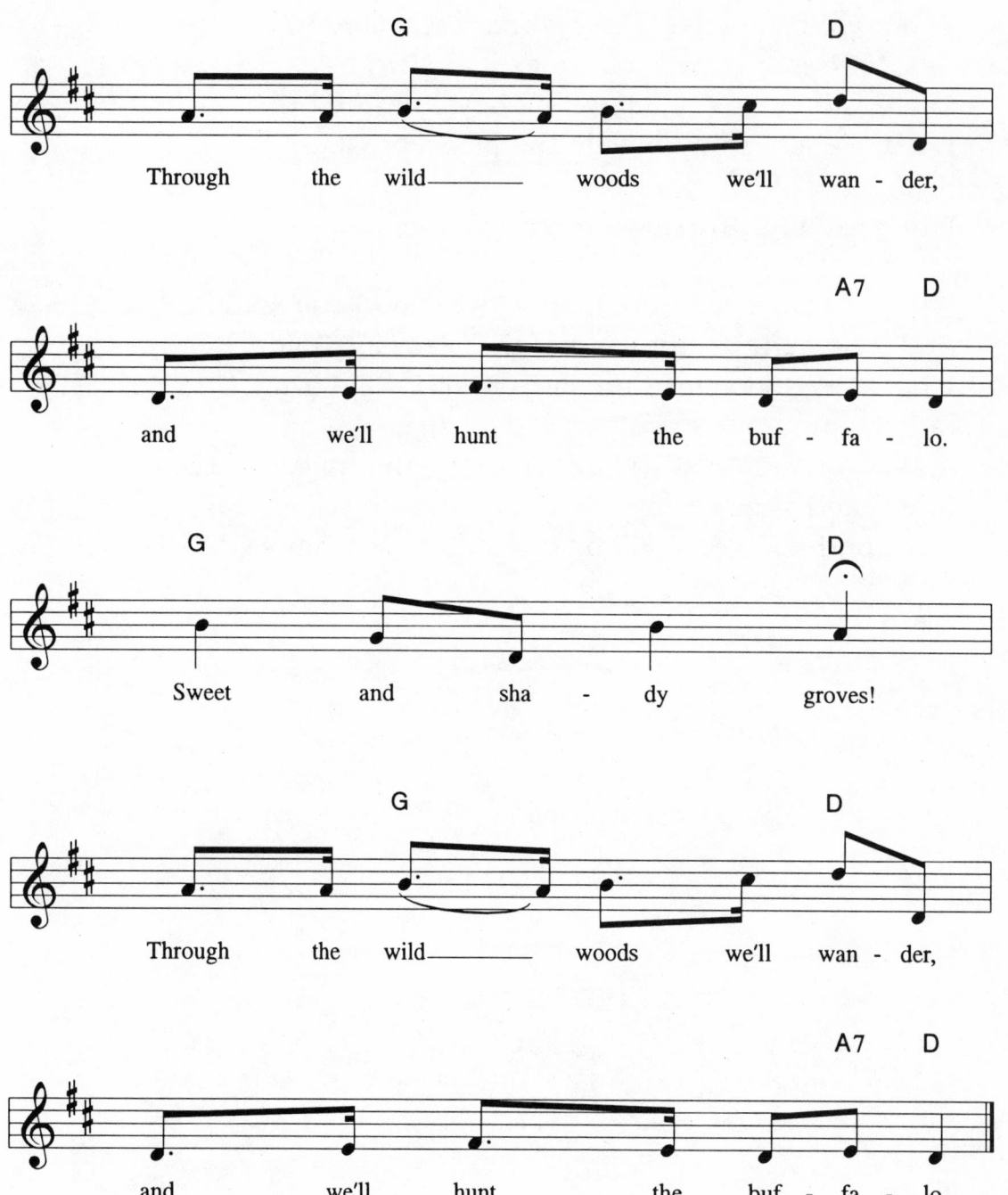

Come all ye fine young women who have got a mind to go,
That you may make us clothing; you may knit and you may sew.
We'll build you fine log cabins in the pleasant Ohio.
Through the wild woods we'll wander, and we'll chase the buffalo.
Sweet and shady groves!
Through the wild woods we'll wander, and we'll chase the buffalo.

There are fishes in the rivers that are suited to our use.
Beside there's lofty sugar trees that yield to us their juice.
There is all kinds of game, my boys, beside the buck and doe,
When we all settle down in the pleasant Ohio.
Sweet and shady groves!
When we all settle down in the pleasant Ohio.

'Tis you can sow and reap, my love, and I can spin and sew
And we'll settle in the land of the pleasant Ohio,
Where the sun shines bright from morn 'till night, and down the
        stream we'll go,
And good and great will be our state, the mighty Ohio!
Sweet and shady groves!
And good and great will be our state, the mighty Ohio!

The presidential election of 1800 was a race beween John Adams, representing the Federalist Party and running on a platform of strong, centralized government, and Thomas Jefferson, representing the Democratic-Republican Party and advocating states' rights. When the electoral votes were counted, the two candidates were tied, so the election of the next President became the responsibility of the House of Representatives. Thomas Jefferson was finally elected on the thirty-sixth ballot on February 17, 1801.

President Jefferson had a strong interest in the westward expansion of the United States. In 1803, he obtained a grant from Congress to support the exploration of the Louisiana Purchase by Meriwether Lewis and George Rogers Clark. In addition, he encouraged the continuing settlement of the Northwest Territory. In April, 1802, Congress passed the Enabling Act which set northern and western boundaries for Ohio and divided it from the rest of the Northwest Territory. This paved the way for statehood, and Ohio became the seventeenth state in the United States on March 1, 1803. Dr. Edward Tiffin was elected the first governor of Ohio, and Chillicothe was designated as the state capital.

"Jefferson and Liberty" is a song which contrasts Jefferson's administration as President with that of his predecessor, John Adams. In seeking to increase federal government control, Adams enacted the Alien and Sedition Acts. The Alien Acts permitted the deportation or imprisonment of any foreign person considered suspicious. The Sedition Act made it a crime to criticize the government, the President, or the Congress. Several journalists who wrote articles sympathetic to Thomas Jefferson were jailed under this act during the Adams administration. This constitutes the "reign of terror" described in the song. The Alien and Sedition Acts were extremely unpopular. After Jefferson became President, these acts, which expired after a set period of time, were not renewed. "Jefferson and Liberty" was a popular song during the early years of Thomas Jefferson's presidency. It celebrated a change in political administrations and was a sort of forerunner of the campaign songs of later presidential elections. The song had a widespread appeal and was undoubtedly known and sung in Ohio around the time that statehood was granted.

JEFFERSON AND LIBERTY

Robert Treat Paine, Jr.   "Gobby-O" (Traditional Irish tune)

The gloom - y night before us flies, The reign of ter - ror now is o'er; Its gags, in - qui - si - tors and spies, Its hordes of har - pies are no more.

CHORUS:

Re - joice, Co - lum - bia's sons, re - joice! To ty - rants nev - er bend your knee, But join with heart and soul and voice, For Jef - fer - son and lib - er - ty.

O'er vast Columbia's varied clime,
Her cities, forests, shores and dales,
In rising majesty sublime,
Immortal liberty prevails.
Chorus

Hail, long expected, glorious day!
Illustrious, memorable morn,
When freedom's fabric from decay
Rebuilds for millions yet unborn.
Chorus

Here strangers from a thousand shores,
Compelled by tyranny to roam,
Shall find, amidst abundant stores,
A nobler and a happier home.
Chorus

Here art shall lift her laureled head,
Wealth, industry and peace divine,
And where dark pathless forests spread,
Rich fields and lofty cities shine.
Chorus

Ohio's entry into the War of 1812 began with the organization of an Ohio militia under the command of General William Hull in May, 1812. This army marched northward and reached Detroit in July, 1812, but the overcautious Hull soon surrendered Detroit to the British. General William Henry Harrison then organized an army made up mostly of Kentucky militiamen to attempt to retake Detroit. Harrison eventually established a headquarters at Fort Meigs on the Maumee River, where he successfully withstood a British siege.

The turning point in the War of 1812 came when a fleet of American ships under the command of Commodore Oliver Hazard Perry defeated a British fleet of approximately the same size in the Battle of Lake Erie. This battle took place on September 10, 1813, and occurred not far from the Bass Islands. The American victory destroyed the British supply lines to Detroit and caused the British to abandon the city and retreat into Canada. General Harrison's troops pursued them and defeated the retreating British army at the Battle of Thames, which was fought near Chatham, Ontario, on October 5, 1813. The Indian leader, Tecumseh, was killed in this battle, resulting in the dissolution of the Indian forces which had supported the British. This battle decisively ended the British threat to Ohio and the Northwest Territory. Approximately 24,500 enlisted men and 1,750 officers from Ohio served in the War of 1812.

"Johnny Has Gone For A Soldier" is a song of Irish origin that was popular during the War of 1812. "Perry's Victory" is a ballad which tells the story of the decisive American victory in the Battle of Lake Erie.

JOHNNY HAS GONE FOR A SOLDIER

Traditional

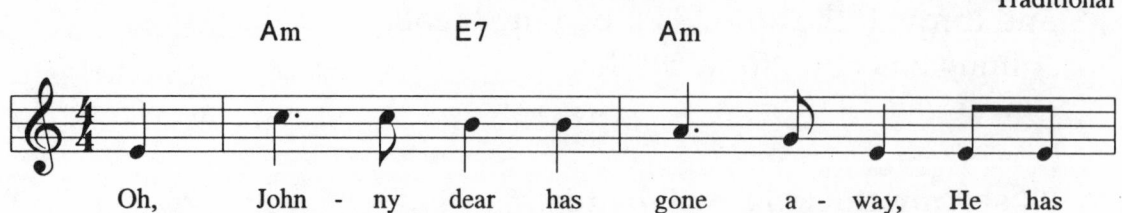

Oh, John - ny dear has gone a - way, He has

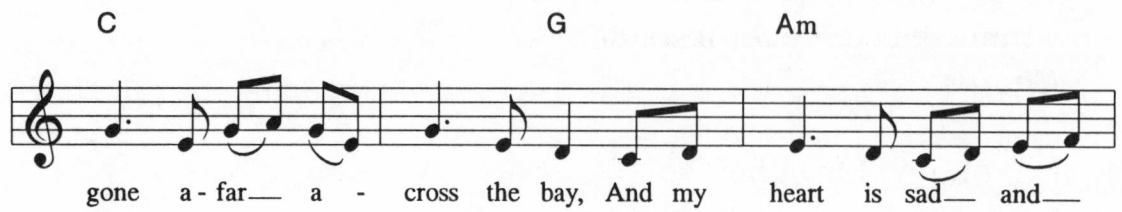

gone a - far— a - cross the bay, And my heart is sad— and—

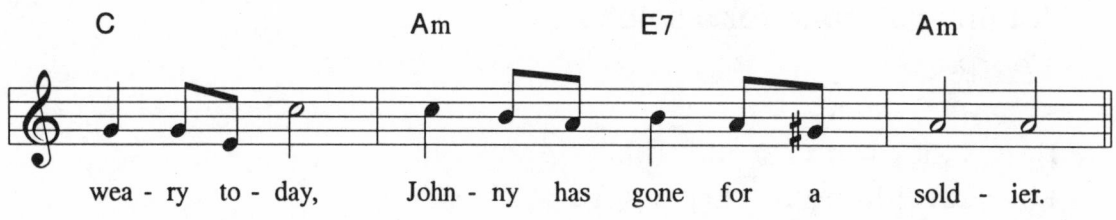

wea - ry to - day, John - ny has gone for a sold - ier.

CHORUS:

Shule, shule, shule a - grah, Time can on - ly

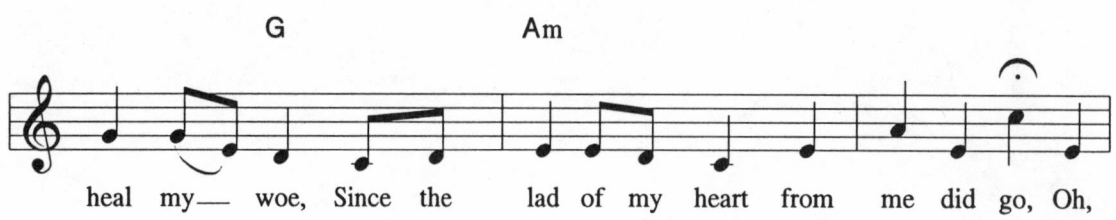

heal my— woe, Since the lad of my heart from me did go, Oh,

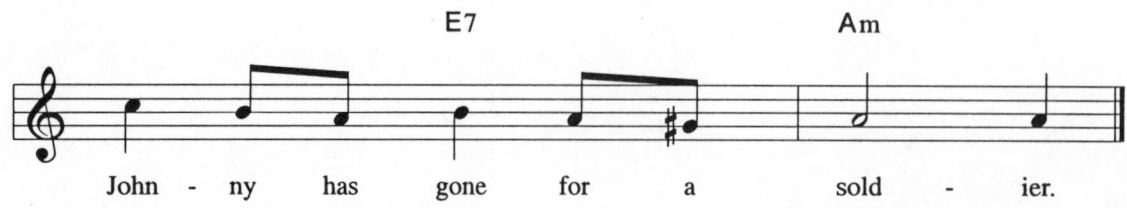

John - ny has gone for a sold - ier.

41

I'll dye my dress, I'll dye it red,
And through the streets I'll beg my bread,
And through the streets I'll beg my bread,
Johnny has gone for a soldier.
Chorus

I'll sell my clock, I'll sell my reel,
I'll sell my flax and my spinning wheel,
To buy my love a sword of steel,
Johnny has gone for a soldier.
Chorus

Me, oh my, I love him so,
Broke my heart to see him go,
Only time can heal my woe,
Johnny has gone for a soldier.
Chorus

Here I sit on Buttermilk Hill,
Who can blame me cry my fill,
And every tear would turn a mill,
Johnny has gone for a soldier.
Chorus

PERRY'S VICTORY

Traditional

Ye tars of Co - lum - bia, give ear to my sto - ry, Who

fought with brave Per - ry where can - nons did roar; Your val - or has

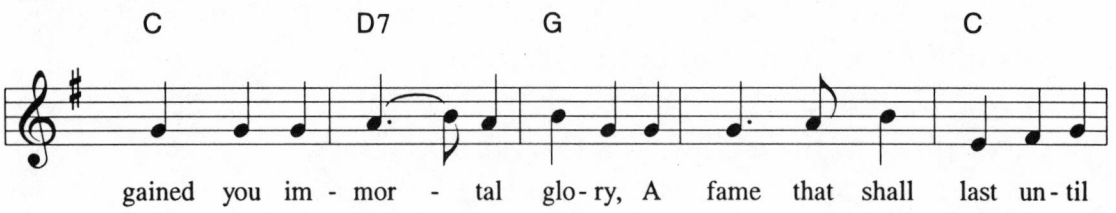

gained you im - mor - tal glo - ry, A fame that shall last un - til

time is no more. Co - lum - bi - an tars are the true sons of

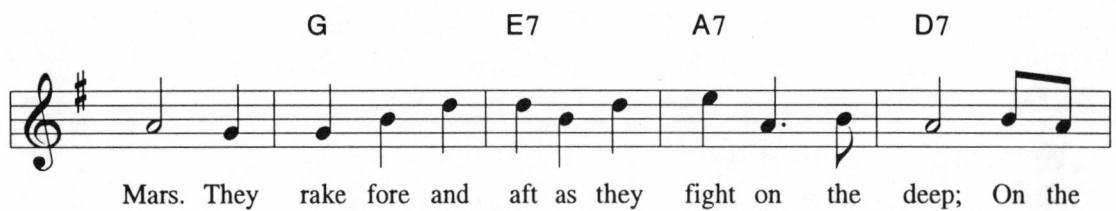

Mars. They rake fore and aft as they fight on the deep; On the

bed of Lake Er - ie com - mand - ed by Per - ry, They

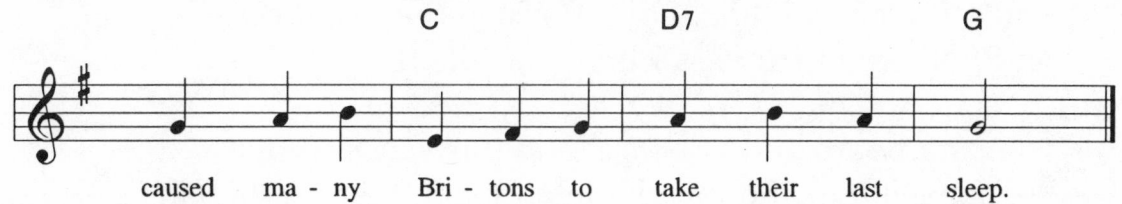

caused ma - ny Bri - tons to take their last sleep.

'Twas just at sunrise, and a glorious day,
Our squadron at anchor, snug in Put-in-Bay;
When we saw the bold Britons and cleared for a bout,
Instead of Put-in, by the Lord, we put out.
Up went Union Jack, never up there before,
"Don't give up the ship!" was the motto it bore;
And as soon as that motto our gallant lads saw,
They thought of their *Lawrence* and shouted, "Huzza!"

O, then, 'twould have raised your hat three inches higher,
To see how we dashed in among them like fire;
The *Lawrence* went first, and the rest as they could,
 And a long time the brunt of the battle she stood.
'Twas peppering work — fire, fury, and smoke —
And groans from the wounded lads spite of them broke;
The water turned red round the ship as she lay,
Though 'twas never before so till that bloody day.

They fell all around us, like spars in a gale,
The shot made a sieve of each rag of a sail;
And out of our crew, scarce a dozen remained,
But these gallant tars still the battle maintained.
'Twas then our Commander — God bless his young heart! —
Thought it best from his well-peppered ship to depart,
And bring up the rest who were lagging behind,
For why? They were sadly in want of a wind.

Whole volleys of muskets were leveled at him,
But the devil a one ever grazed e'en a limb,
Though he stood up erect in the stern of the boat,
Till the crew pulled him down by the skirts of his coat.
At length, through Heaven's mercy, we reached the other ship,
And the wind springing up, we gave her the whip,
And ran down the line, boys, through thick and through thin,
And bothered their ears with a horrible din.

Then starboard and larboard, and this way and that,
We banged 'em and raked 'em and laid their masts flat;
Till one after the other they hauled down their flag,
And an end put for that time to Johnny Bull's brag.
The *Detroit*, *Queen Charlotte*, and *Lady Prevost*,
Not able to fight or run, gave up the ghost;
And not one of them all from our grapplings got free,
Though we'd just fifty-four guns and they'd sixty-three.

OLIVER HAZARD PERRY

The Ohio River was the main avenue by which pioneer settlement came to Ohio after the Revolutionary War. Many early pioneers floated down the Ohio River on flatboats bound for such early settlements as Marietta or Cincinnati. The flatboats usually made a one-way trip and were torn apart for their lumber when a party reached its destination.

The earliest commercial boats on the Ohio River were the keelboats. Keelboats were usually about twelve feet wide and thirty feet long. They were made of wood, and the main body of the boat was covered with a roof to protect the cargo from rain. The average keelboat carried up to forty tons of freight. The keelboat had narrow platforms called running-boards along each side where the crew worked. A keelboat crew usually numbered from six to eighteen men, commanded by a captain. The keelboats were propelled by poling done by the crew (half on each side of the boat). They had to remain near the shore of the river where the water was shallow, and the poles would touch the bottom. Keelboats could be propelled both up and down the river in this manner. Each boat also had a large oar at the back which served as a rudder for steering. The flatboat and keelboat era on the Ohio River lasted from the 1780's until about 1820.

"Shawneetown" describes a keelboat trip down the Ohio River to Shawneetown, an early commercial settlement in southern Illinois. "Working on a Pushboat" gives insight into the life of the keelboatman. The song describes such frequent occurrences as working in the rain, getting stuck on a sandbar, and thinking about a woman in the next port of call. "Nancy Till" is a song about a boatman who serenades the girl he loves as he tries to convince her to run away with him.

SHAWNEETOWN

Traditional

Some—— rows—— up, but we—— floats—— down,

Way down the O - hi - o to—— Shaw - nee - town.

CHORUS:

And it's hard on the beech oar; she moves too slow,

Way down to Shaw - nee - town on the O - hi - o.

Now the current's got her, and we'll take up the slack,
Float her down to Shawneetown, and we'll bushwhack her back.
Chorus

The whiskey's in the jug, boys; the wheat is in the sack.
We'll trade 'em down to Shawneetown, and we'll bring the rock salt back.
Chorus

The water's mighty warm, boys; the air is cold and dank,
And the cursed fog, it gets so thick you cannot see the bank.
Chorus

WORKING ON A PUSHBOAT

Traditional

Work - ing on a push - boat,

From Cat - letts - burg to Pike,

Work - ing on a push - boat,

For old man Jef - frey Zike,

For old man Jef - frey Zike.

48

Working on a pushboat,
Water's mighty slack,
Taking sorghum molasses down,
And bringing sugar back,
And bringing sugar back.

Pushing mighty hard, boys,
Sand bar's in the way;
Working like a son-of-a-gun
For mighty scanty pay,
For mighty scanty pay.

Working on a pushboat,
Fifty cents a day.
I'll buy a dress for Cynthy Jane.
I'll throw the rest away,
I'll throw the rest away.

I wish I had a nickel.
I wish I had a dime.
I'd spend it all on Cynthy Jane.
I'd dress her mighty fine.
I'd dress her mighty fine.

Weather's mighty hot, boys,
Got blisters on my feet,
Working on a pushboat,
To buy my bread and meat,
To buy my bread and meat.

Working on a pushboat,
Working in the rain;
When I get to Catlettsburg,
Goodbye old Cynthy Jane,
Goodbye old Cynthy Jane.

NANCY TILL

White's Serenaders (1851)

Down in the cane - brake, close by the mill,

There lived a pret - ty girl; her name was Nan - cy Till. She

knew that I loved her; she knew it long. I'm

going to ser - e - nade her and I'll sing— this— song.

CHORUS:

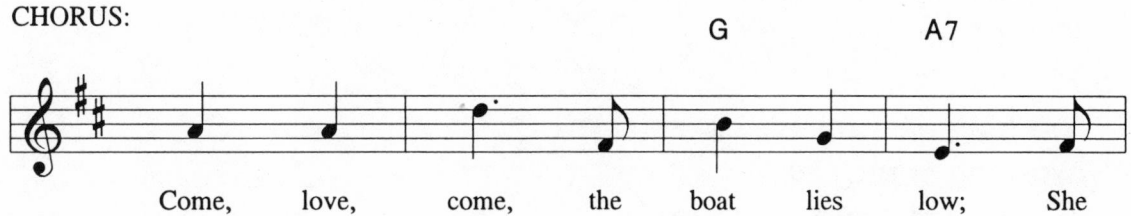

Come, love, come, the boat lies low; She

50

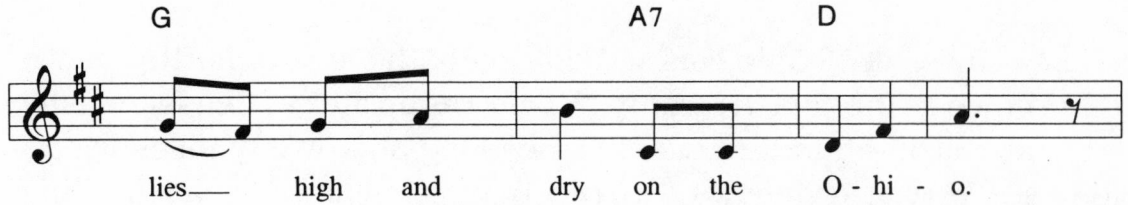

lies— high and dry on the O - hi - o.

Come, love, come, won't you come a - long with me?

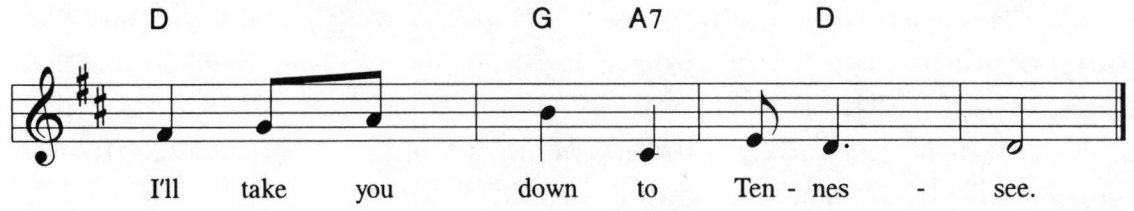

I'll take you down to Ten - nes - see.

Open the window, love, oh, do!
And listen to the music that I play for you.
The whisperings of love, so soft and low,
I'll harmonize my voice with the old banjo.
Chorus

Farewell, love, I must now away,
I've a long way to travel before the break of day.
The next time I come, be ready, love, to go,
A-sailing on the banks of the Ohio.
Chorus

By 1820, all of Ohio was settled except the area of northwestern Ohio known as the "Black Swamp." (This was an area of dense, marshy forest about one hundred twenty miles long and twenty miles wide.) Pioneer life was giving way to the development of small farming communities throughout the state. Northern Ohio was settled mainly by people from New England and Pennsylvania, while large sections of southern Ohio were settled by pioneers of Scotch-Irish origin who were from Virginia and Kentucky. These early settlers were nearly all farmers. The most important crops raised were corn and wheat, but rye, buckwheat, barley, hay, and tobacco were also grown.

As late as the 1840's, roads in Ohio were very primitive and were often impassable after heavy rains. Consequently, most early settlements developed along the rivers (and, later, along the canals). Water transportation during this time was far more reliable than was land transportation. The first steamboats were developed around the time of the War of 1812, and the *Orleans* became the first steamboat to travel on the Ohio River when it made its maiden voyage in 1811. In 1818, another early steamboat, *Walk-in-the-Water*, was the first steamboat to cross Lake Erie, traveling from Buffalo to Detroit with stops in Cleveland and Sandusky. The early steamboats had a maximum speed of eight miles per hour. By 1819, there were sixty-three steamboats working on the Ohio River, some being freight hauling boats and others carrying passengers. The heyday of the steamboat era was from 1840 to 1860, and many of the passenger boats were very lavish and ornate.

During the period from 1820 to 1850, agriculture remained the mainstay of life in Ohio, but commerce gradually increased in importance. "On The Banks Of The Ohio" presents a pastoral picture of life on a small farm along the Ohio River during this time. The song was written and sung by the Nightingale Serenaders, a traveling musical group which performed on the steamboats that plied the waters of the Ohio River during the middle nineteenth century.

ON THE BANKS OF THE OHIO

Nightingale Serenaders

We— live on the banks of the O - hi - o,

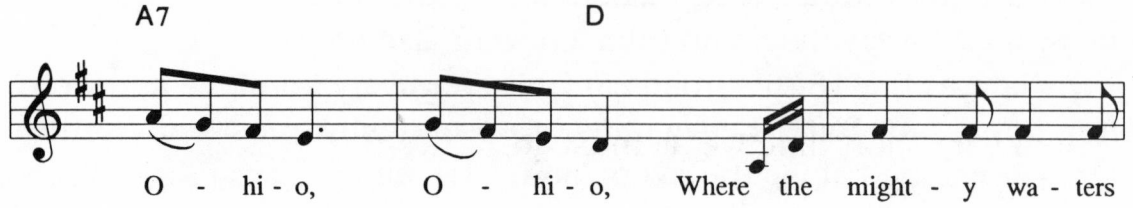

O - hi - o, O - hi - o, Where the might - y wa - ters

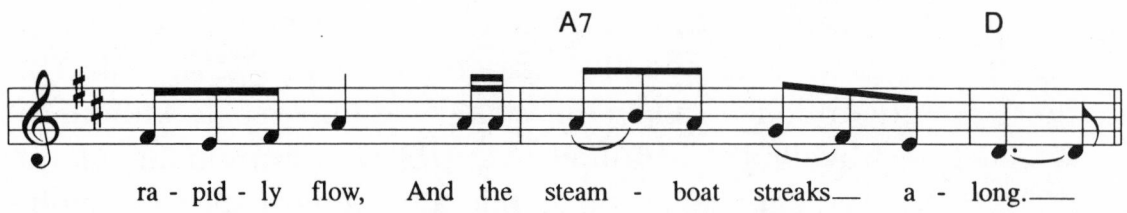

ra - pid - ly flow, And the steam - boat streaks— a - long.—

CHORUS:

We— live on the banks of the O - hi - o,

O - hi - o, O - hi - o, We— live on the banks of the

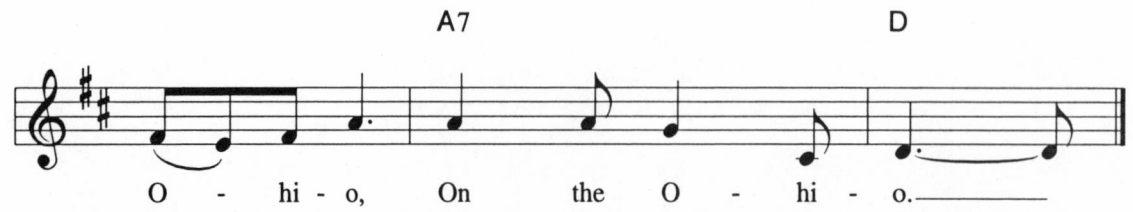

O - hi - o, On the O - hi - o.—

When day is gone and our work is done,
Ohio, Ohio,
To our cabins we go and have our fun,
Sweet music we exercise.
Chorus

Drop not fellows as we hoe,
Ohio, Ohio,
Tilling the banks of the Ohio,
To raise the tobacco and corn.
Chorus

In a very short time we all must go,
Ohio, Ohio,
Back to the banks of the Ohio,
To the homes we love so well.
Chorus

After the War of 1812, interest in the creation of canal systems developed in several states. Roads were few and poor, and canals were seen as the most feasible way to move people and goods from one place to another. The Erie Canal in New York, which ran from Albany to Lake Erie, was completed in 1825. Its success prompted other states, including Ohio, to develop plans for canal systems. Digging for the Ohio and Erie Canal, which ran from Cleveland to Portsmouth, was begun in 1825. The canal was completed in 1832 and was 308 miles long with 153 locks. The Miami and Erie Canal was completed from Cincinnati to Dayton in 1828 and was finally totally completed in 1845 when it was connected to the Wabash and Erie Canal at Defiance. It was 249 miles long with 106 locks. Along with the construction of these two main canals, several branch canals were also built in various parts of the state. In addition, several reservoirs were built throughout the state to feed the canals.

The Ohio canals operated about eight months of the year (April through November) and were closed and drained in the winter. In spring, reservoir gates were opened, and the canals refilled rapidly.

The primary function for which the canals were built was the transport of freight. Canalboats carried all kinds of cargo — lumber, wheat, corn, flour, oats, barley, whiskey, coal, salt, and so on. However, passenger travel on the canals soon developed as well. Passenger boats were called packets and were constructed in similar style to the freight boats. Canal travel was quite inexpensive. A four day trip from Cleveland to Portsmouth in the 1830's cost $1.85 including meals.

The size of the canalboats was determined by both canal and lock dimensions. The canals were forty feet wide at the top, twenty-six feet wide at the bottom, and four feet deep. The average lock was built of stone or timber and was ninety feet long by fifteen feet wide. The lift averaged six to twelve feet per lock, and a lock could be filled or emptied in about ten minutes. Canalboats were pulled by two to six mules or horses which walked along the towpath on the bank of the canal. In 1830, a speed limit of four miles per hour was set for the Ohio canals because it had been determined that boats going any faster than that eroded the earthen walls of the canals.

The Ohio canal era reached its height in the 1840's. The advent of the railroads brought about the slow decline of the canals beginning in the 1850's. By the 1890's, many of the smaller canals had closed, and

there was little traffic on the canals. The last operating sections of the Ohio and Erie and Miami and Erie Canals were closed in 1913 after having sustained heavy damage in the disastrous January flood of that year.

"The Old Skipper," "Fairy Palace," "The Mules Ran Off," "That Old Towpath," and "Last Trip In The Fall" were all written by Pearl R. Nye, who left a legacy of Ohio canal songs. Pearl Nye was born into a family of canallers in 1872. He and his eight brothers all became canalboat men, and he continued to work on the Ohio and Erie Canal until it closed. Nye wrote over one hundred songs about life on the canals. Many of his songs, such as "That Old Towpath," extol the beauty of the natural world along the canals, while providing a somewhat romanticized but fascinating picture of canal life. "Fairy Palace" describes a trip from Cleveland to Portsmouth (referred to in the song as the Rainbow Town). Towns and sights all along the way are mentioned in the song's many verses. "The Mules Ran Off" is based on an actual incident from Nye's canal experiences when his mules were frightened by a thunderstorm.

THE OLD SKIPPER

Pearl R. Nye

"Whiskey Waltz"

I'm an old canal - boat skip - per with black snake in hand, So fare you well dar - ling my mules will not stand. The line's on the dead - eye, for Ports - mouth I'm bound. I love the old tow - path, best place I have found.

I've been on the lakes and the rivers, Oh boy,
But my dear Silver Ribbon is the place I enjoy.
'Tis a place oh so matchless, each day new things born,
And I love to boat wheat and the big yellow corn.

There's tanbark and hooppoles, wet goods, merchandise,
Clay, coal, brick and lumber, cordwood, stone and ice.
Yes, all that was needed, we boated, dear Pal,
Best time of our lives we had on the canal.

I will not be a rover, for I love my boat,
I am happy, contented, yet work, dream and float.
My mules are not hungry; they're lively and gay.
The plank is pulled in; we are off on our way.

FAIRY PALACE

Pearl R. Nye

"On the Banks of Salee"

We're go - ing south to - mor - row, Dear, But, oh, what times and fun,—— We'll have en route to Ports - mouth, 'Tis a grand and glor - ious run. But we'll run a - long to - geth - er, Dear, How hap - py we will be, On our lit - tle Fai - ry Pal - ace, Where we'll be so gay and free.——

In Akron we will lay over,
Yes, for a day or two,
She's a romping gay old town,
For there's much that's strange and new. *Chorus*

There's many bright historic spots,
That often give you thrills,
But you'll wonder all along,
Shipyards, warehouses, mills. *Chorus*

At Massillon we have gay times;
Navarre is blessed with coal;
Bolivar's historic fame,
Will stir your very soul. *Chorus*

Zoar, Zoar loves the canal,
Women, children did much work;
Baskets, buckets, anything,
Yes, they helped remove the dirt. *Chorus*

At Canal Dover you will smile,
Also in Trenton, too,
Lock Seventeen and Old Blue Hole,
You will ne'er forget these views. *Chorus*

Newcomerstown, Coshocton,
Past Roscoe, interesting, true.
You will often speak of them,
And the world will seem like new. *Chorus*

At coal port Dresden and Newark,
Reservoir, Hebron, too,
Sights and things you'll ne'er forget,
And the scenery ever new. *Chorus*

At Baltimore and Basil,
Carroll, Lockville, so gay,

Canal Winchester, Groveport, Straight,
Oh, of them there's much to say. *Chorus*

Lockbourne's big distillery,
Columbus, endless chain;
Circleville, so gay and cute,
You will love to see again. *Chorus*

There's Chillicothe, sure is bright!
Oh, yes, a real canal town;
'Tis no joke we always stop,
Though we're headed up or down. *Chorus*

In Crooked Creek at Waverly,
Also her lazy slip,
At the big distillery,
Most turtles of the trip. *Chorus*

At Sunfish Creek, the largest spring,
In all the Buckeye State.
This Ribbon Route's most beautiful,
You'll praise and oft relate. *Chorus*

The largest vine that's in the world,
Is found near in these parts.
A sycamore at Lucasville,
So large, it jars the heart. *Chorus*

Katydids and locusts, crickets,
Birds, oh, all serenade,
From Cleveland to our Rainbow Town,
Then who should be afraid? *Chorus*

So we'll enjoy it all along,
And what things you will behold!
The canal is so entrancing,
'Tis a life that ne'er grows old. *Chorus*

THE MULES RAN OFF

Pearl R. Nye

"Oh! Susanna" (Stephen Foster)

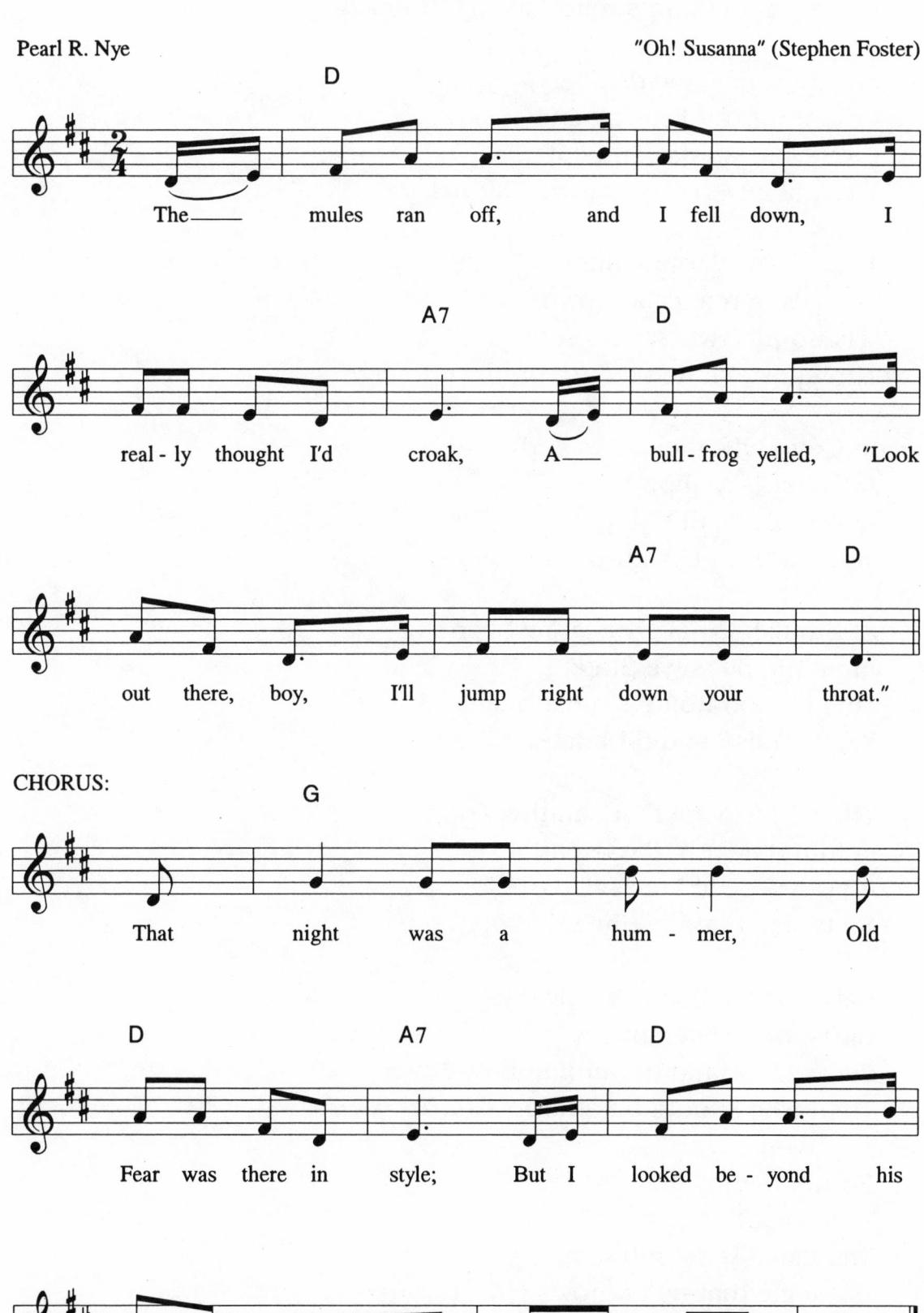

The—— mules ran off, and I fell down, I real-ly thought I'd croak, A—— bull-frog yelled, "Look out there, boy, I'll jump right down your throat."

CHORUS:

That night was a hum-mer, Old Fear was there in style; But I looked be-yond his ca-pers, For I love my old ca-nal.

I sure felt funny, yes I did;
'Twas muddy, all was wet;
And everything that had a voice,
I seem to hear them yet.
Chorus

The turtles, fish, would splash about
Muskrats, mink, dive and swim,
And every step I took that night,
Old Fear would smile and grin.
Chorus

The mules I found in waiting,
While our craft did gently float;
The rain soon came in torrents,
And we jumped into the boat.
Chorus

Next morning all was bright and clear,
The birds would smile in song,
Yes, endless serenading
In turn, the whole day long.
Chorus

THAT OLD TOWPATH

Pearl R. Nye

"The Old Oaken Bucket" (George Kiallmark)

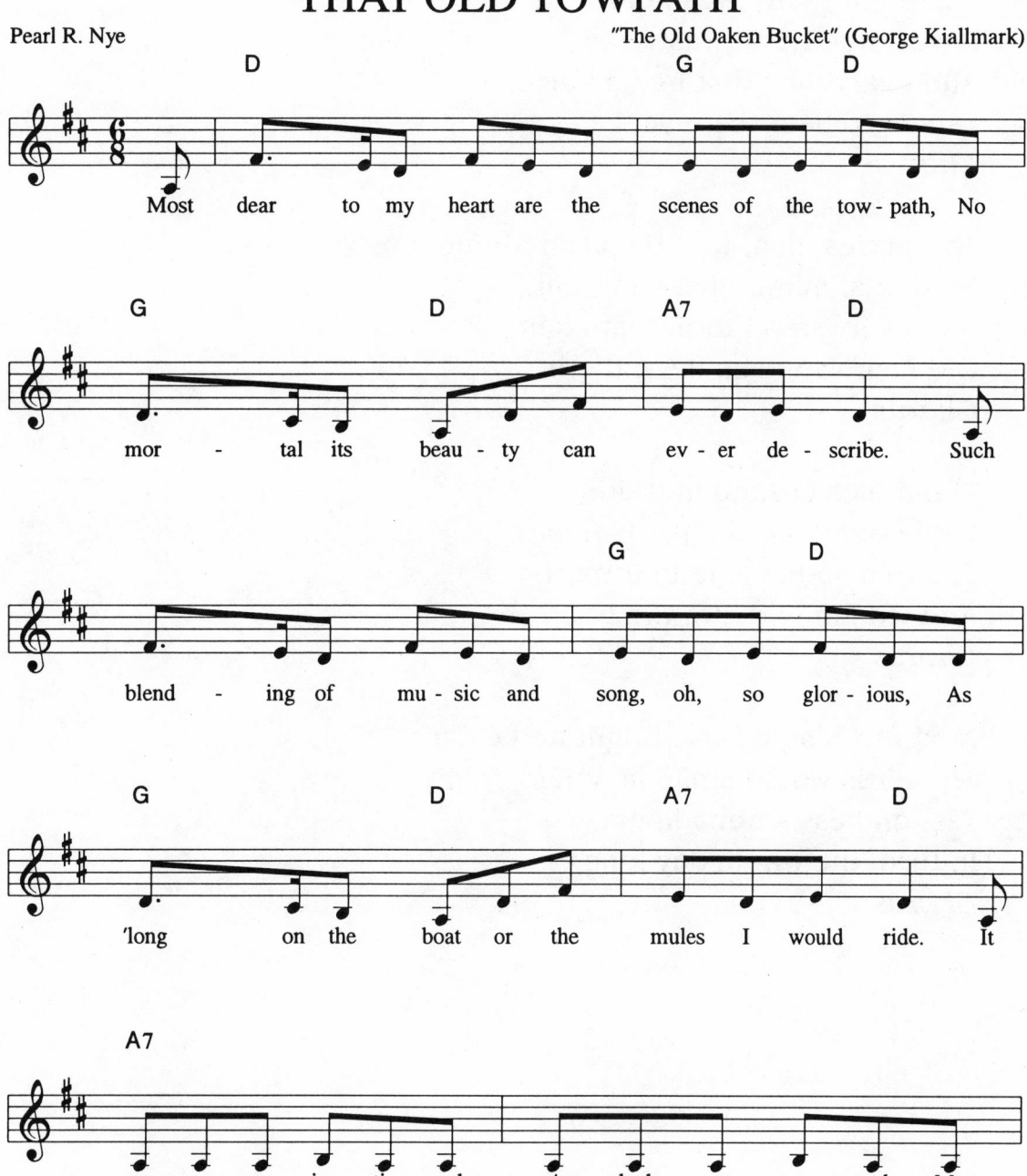

Most dear to my heart are the scenes of the tow-path, No
mor - tal its beau - ty can ev - er de - scribe. Such
blend - ing of mu - sic and song, oh, so glor - ious, As
'long on the boat or the mules I would ride. It
was so ma - jes - tic and ne'er had an e - qual; My

soul in its rap - ture would burst out in song. While

na - ture would smile ev - ery - thing full of laugh - ter, A

won - der - ful pic - ture, as we'd glide a - long!

CHORUS:

That beau - ti - ful tow - path, such splen - dor, so glor - ious, With

dear Mo - ther Na - ture I'd ram - ble a - long.

Upon that old towpath, oh, I was so happy;
Most free of all mortals, the world ever knew;
I'd love to go back and remain there forever;
'Twas so unexcelling, most beautiful, true;
The air was so freighted with fragrance from flowers;
The moss, honey locust, clover, new-mown hay,
And, oh, nature's song, in what glee, she would greet us,
No picture so grand as she, would there display.
Chorus

Upon that old towpath, 'twas heaven, such glory
As barefoot I'd revel in fun, laughter, song;
The snakes would uncoil, make a streak for the water,
The frogs jump and "chug," turtles waddle along.
Those wonderful trees, bowing, waving, so graceful,
The elms and willows, the sycamore, pines,
The elders and alders, yes, all of their kindred
And even our timid friend, Mrs. Grape Vine.
Chorus

The hills, valleys, creeks, rivers, yes, all were with them,
They'd smile, sing and dance, 'twas an excellent scene.
I'd give all the world, yes, and what e'er my future,
If I could live over this wonderful dream.
No place in creation can ever approach it;
The Lord set His seal on it, beautiful, grand;
'Twas God, man, and nature all working together,
A handiwork, marvelous, water and land.
Chorus

LAST TRIP IN THE FALL

Pearl R. Nye   "Between Me and the Wall"

At Nick Hert's mine near Tren - ton, Where we put on eight - y tons, Seemed

ev - ery - thing was right a - bout, No mat - ter where we'd turn, But

we kept on a - mov - ing, For we must heed dut - y's call; And

land - ed safe in Cleve - land, Where we laid up for the fall.

Window-glass ice was everywhere,
We handled lines with gloves,
They soon were wet, our hands so cold,
And that nobody loves;
But soon we were all winter-set,
O yes, were feeling fine,
And eating nuts while cracking jokes
Of things along the line.

That winter was the limit, O yes,
For us Big Ditch boys;
Had everything at our command
That city folk enjoy.
No matter how the cards would run,
My heart would sing and smile;
I learned these things, yes, years ago
Upon the old canal.

But who in God's creation
Can enumerate this life?
'Tis so unique and lovely
Where the heart is free from strife.
I'm died in wool a Canaler;
I don't care what be the sky,
I'll stay upon the Great Big Ditch
Until the day I die!

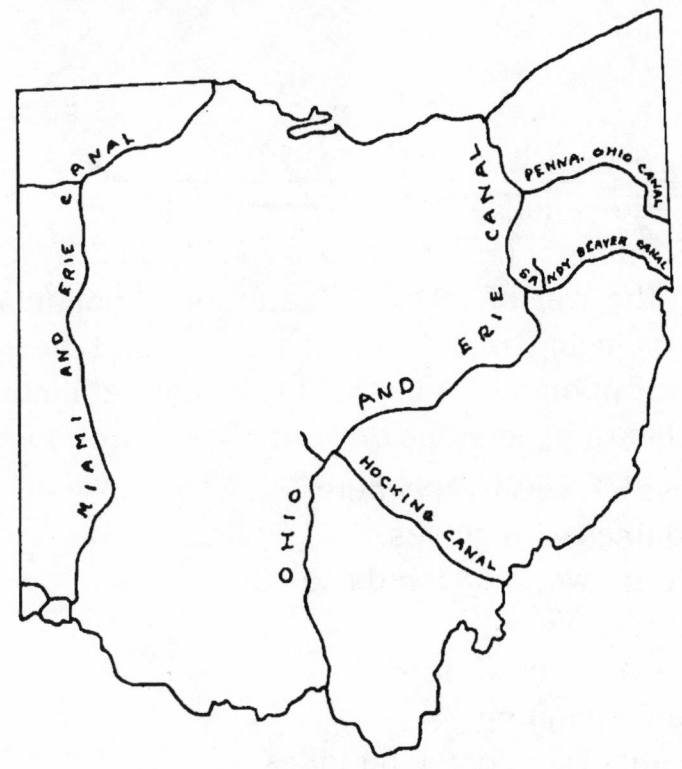

The presidential campaign of 1840 pitted the incumbent President Martin Van Buren (a Democrat) against William Henry Harrison (a Whig). Although Van Buren had defeated Harrison in the election of 1836, his popularity had been eroded by the economic crisis of the Panic of 1837. In the vigorous campaign of 1840, songs first played an important part in campaign politics.

William Henry Harrison, an Ohioan who was born in Virginia, was victorious in the election, but his presidency was short-lived. He caught a cold and developed pneumonia after delivering his inaugural address in the rain. He died a month after he became President.

OLD TIPPECANOE

The song "Old Tippecanoe" was set to the traditional tune "Rosin the Beau." Harrison's nickname, "Old Tippecanoe," was given to him as the result of his victory over the Indians in the Battle of Tippecanoe, which took place in what is now Indiana in 1811. The song extols Harrison's war record and his leadership at the Battle of Thames (in Ontario) during the War of 1812. Like modern politicians, those in 1840 enjoyed "slinging mud" at each other and besmirching the reputation of the opponent. Thus, "Old Tippecanoe" includes a couple of stanzas which cast aspersions on Martin Van Buren because he was a gentleman farmer, rather than having been a valiant soldier like Harrison.

OLD TIPPECANOE

Anonymous

"Rosin the Beau"

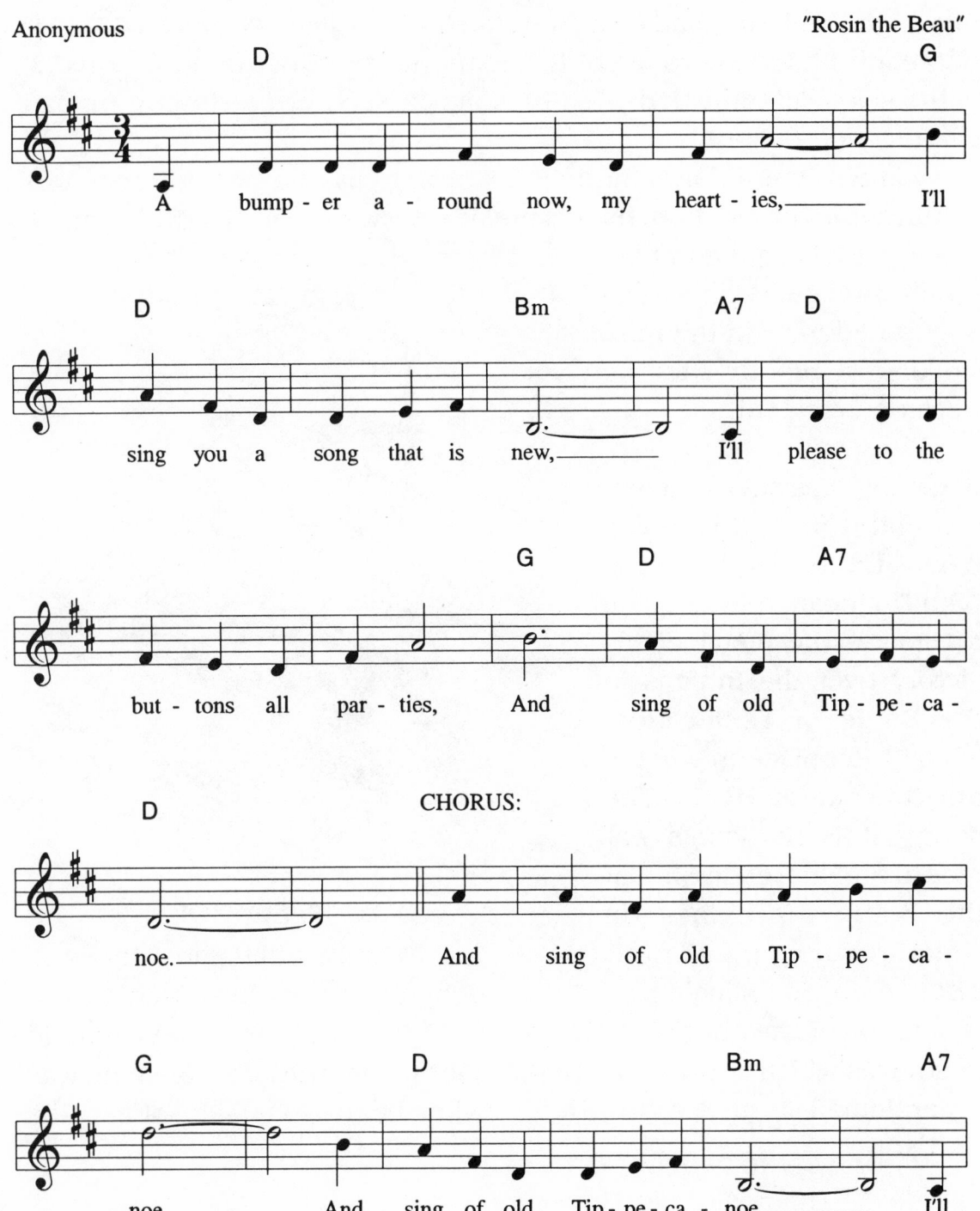

A bump-er a-round now, my heart-ies,_____ I'll
sing you a song that is new,_____ I'll please to the
but-tons all par-ties, And sing of old Tip-pe-ca-
noe._____ And sing of old Tip-pe-ca-
noe,_____ And sing of old Tip-pe-ca-noe,_____ I'll

please to the but - tons all par - ties, And

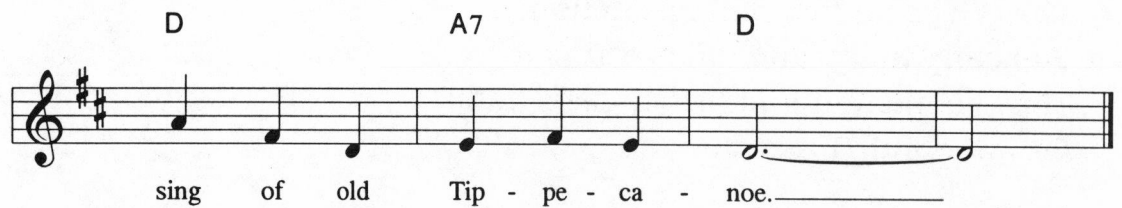

sing of old Tip - pe - ca - noe.

When first near the Thames' gentle waters,
My sword for my country I drew,
I fought for America's daughters,
'Long side of old Tippecanoe.

Chorus:
'Long side of old Tippecanoe,
'Long side of old Tippecanoe,
I fought for America's daughters,
'Long side of old Tippecanoe.

And who pray is Martin Van Buren,
What wonders did he ever do?
Was he in the Battle of Orleans,
Meigs, Thames or old Tippecanoe?

Chorus:
Meigs, Thames or old Tippecanoe,
Meigs, Thames or old Tippecanoe,
Was he in the Battle or Orleans,
Meigs, Thames or old Tippecanoe?

Oh, no, he had no taste for fighting,
Such rough work he never could do,
He shirked it off on to brave Jackson,
And the hero of Tippecanoe.

Chorus:
The hero of Tippecanoe,
The hero of Tippecanoe,
He shirked it off on to brave Jackson,
And the hero of Tippecanoe.

The Whigs at the coming election,
Will carry their candidates through,
They've made the judicious selection
Of Tyler and Tippecanoe.

Chorus:
Of Tyler and Tippecanoe,
Of Tyler and Tippecanoe,
They've made the judicious selection
Of Tyler and Tippecanoe.

The Wyandots were one of several Indian tribes who lived in Ohio at the time that pioneer settlement began. The Wyandots spoke an Iroquoian language and were actually a splinter group of the Huron tribe. During the middle seventeenth century, the Hurons lived in the Georgian Bay area of Canada, but in 1649, they were attacked and defeated by the Iroquois, who sought to control the lucrative fur trade in the region. The defeated Huron bands moved farther west into what is now Michigan and Wisconsin. In the early 1700's, when Iroquois influence in the Ohio country weakened, the Wyandots gradually moved into the area and settled initially along the Maumee and Sandusky Rivers.

The Wyandots continued to live in north central Ohio throughout the period of pioneer settlement. A few Wyandots fought with the British during the War of 1812, but most were loyal to the Americans. Following the War of 1812, most of the Ohio Wyandots took up residence in the area of Upper Sandusky. In 1816, Reverend John Stewart founded a Methodist mission among these Wyandots. The number of converts grew quite rapidly, and a school was started in connection with the mission in 1821. Most of the Wyandots adopted relatively settled lives as farmers. The tribe also ran a flour mill on the Sandusky River.

During the presidency of Andrew Jackson (1829-1837), a policy was adopted by the federal government to remove all Indians in the eastern United States to reservations west of the Mississippi River. The 674 Wyandots at Upper Sandusky were the last Ohio Indian group to be removed. They were forced to leave their homes and farms and move west in 1843. By that time all of Ohio's other Indian groups had been moved to Kansas or Oklahoma. "The Wyandotte Farewell Song" is a romanticized portrayal of the plight of the Wyandots and of their forced removal from their farms along the Sandusky River and Tymochtee and Brokensword Creeks.

THE WYANDOTTE FAREWELL SONG

James Rankin

"Fare Ye Well, Inniskillen"

A - dieu to the graves— where my fa - thers now
rest! For I must be go - ing a - far to the
West; I've sold my pos - ses - sions; my heart's filled with
woe, To think I must lose— them. A - las, I must go.

Farewell, ye tall oaks, in whose pleasant green shade
In childhood I rambled, in innocence played;
My dog and my hatchet, my arrows and bow,
Are still in remembrance. Alas, I must go.

Adieu, ye loved scenes which bind me like chains,
Where on my gay pony I chased o'er the plains;
The deer and the turkey I tracked in the snow,
But now I must leave them. Alas, I must go.

Adieu to the trails which for many a year
I have traveled to spy out the turkey and deer;
The hills, trees, and flowers that pleased me so
I must leave now forever. Alas, I must go.

Sandusky, Tymochtee, and Brokensword streams
Nevermore shall I see you except in my dreams;
Adieu to the marshes where the cranberries grow,
O'er the great Mississippi, alas, I must go.

The United Society of Believers in Christ's Second Appearing originated in Manchester, England, in 1747, developing originally from a dissident group of Quakers. This group, under the leadership of Ann Lee, acquired the nickname Shakers, due to the unstructured and emotional nature of their religious services in which participants sometimes trembled with emotion. The main body of Shakers, including Ann Lee, emigrated to America in 1774 and settled near Albany, New York.

Communal organization and celibacy were two of the most important aspects of Shaker life. As a result of the celibacy requirement, the Shakers acquired new members exclusively through conversion. However, during the years following the American Revolution, the Shakers enjoyed moderate success in making converts, and by 1800, eleven Shaker settlements with 1,600 members were functioning in New York, Massachusetts, Connecticut, New Hampshire, and Maine.

Shaker growth continued during the first part of the nineteenth century, and four Shaker settlements were founded in Ohio at Union Village (located three miles west of present-day Lebanon), North Union (located eight miles east of Cleveland), Watervliet (located six miles southeast of Dayton), and Whitewater (located in northwestern Hamilton County). Shaker membership reached a high point of around 6,000 in the late 1840's, but thereafter, membership began to decline. There were still about 1,000 Shakers in 1900, but today only a few Shakers, mostly elderly, live in two villages (Canterbury, New Hampshire and Sabbathday Lake, Maine).

The Shakers were known for their highly structured and organized villages, their simple, but well-constructed furniture, and their mechanical and agricultural inventions. Their religious beliefs included a conviction of the unity of the Godhead made whole through the harmonizing of duality and thus combining masculine and feminine elements equally, belief in the ongoing nature of spiritual revelation, and emphasis on the importance of celibacy for the achievement of the highest spiritual life.

The Shakers are also known today for their hymns. Various individual Shakers wrote over one hundred hymns, many of which were reported to have been divinely inspired. The best known hymn is "Simple Gifts." Its words extol the simplicity and beauty of the Shaker life, and its message of gentleness and love can be an inspiration to anyone.

SIMPLE GIFTS

Traditional Shaker hymn

'Tis a gift to be sim - ple, 'tis a

gift to be free, 'Tis a gift to come down

where we ought to be, And when we find our - selves___ in the

place just___ right, We will be in the val - ley of

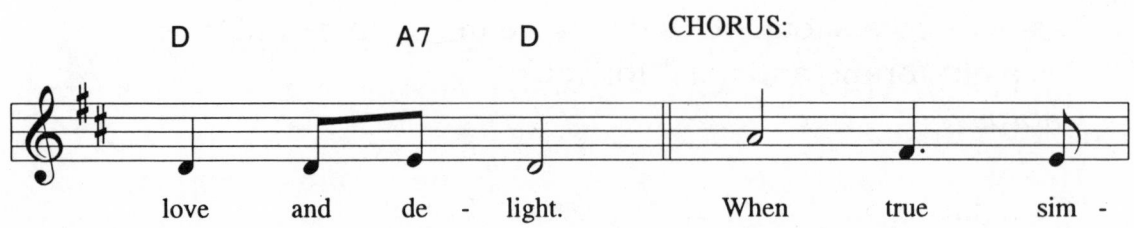

love and de - light. When true sim -

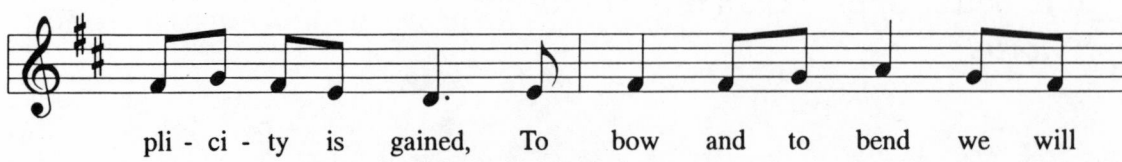

pli - ci - ty is gained, To bow and to bend we will

not be a - shamed. To turn— and to turn— will—

be our de - light, 'Til by turn - ing, turn - ing, we

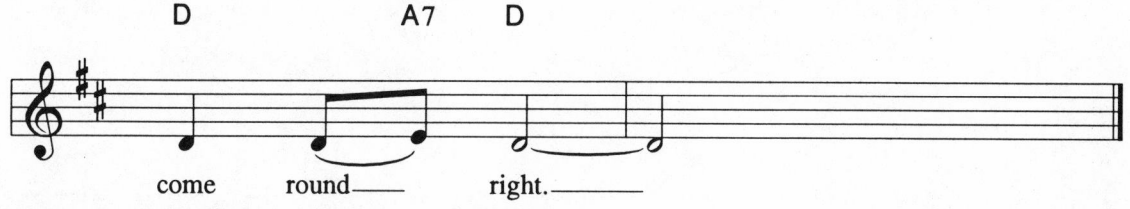

come round— right.—

'Tis a gift to be gentle, 'tis a gift to be fair,
'Tis a gift to wake and breathe the morning air,
To walk every day in the path that we choose,
'Tis a gift we pray we may never, never lose.
Chorus

'Tis a gift to be knowing, 'tis a gift to be kind,
'Tis a gift to wait to hear someone else's mind,
That when we speak our feelings we might come out true,
'Tis a gift for me and a gift for you.
Chorus

'Tis a gift to be loving, 'tis the best gift of all,
Like a warm spring rain bringing beauty when it falls,
And as we use this gift we might come to believe
It is better to give than it is to receive.
Chorus

Anti-slavery sentiment was generally present in Ohio from the time of its founding, and the first abolitionist society in the state was organized at St. Clairsville in 1815 by Benjamin Lundy. During the 1830's, the issue of slavery continued to come under intense scrutiny. The American Antislavery Society was formed in New York in 1833, and several chapters soon were started in Ohio.

As a result of its anti-slavery stance, Ohio became one of the main escape routes for runaway slaves from the South who were attempting to reach freedom in Canada. The Underground Railroad was a loosely organized system designed to provide safe passage through Ohio to runaway slaves. A large number of Ohioans with abolitionist leanings supported the Underground Railroad and aided runaway slaves from the 1830's until the Civil War. Once runaway slaves had crossed the Ohio River, they were housed, fed, and then transported to the next "station" or safe location to the north by sympathetic Ohioans. There were at least twenty-three major crossing points along the Ohio River, and from these, most runaway slaves endeavored to reach one of the five major Lake Erie port towns — Toledo, Sandusky, Cleveland, Fairport Harbor, or Ashtabula — from which boat transportation to Canada could be procured.

BENJAMIN LUNDY

"Follow The Drinking Gourd" is a traditional song giving encouragement to escaped slaves in their flight to the North. The "drinking gourd" referred to is the Big Dipper. Most runaway slaves hid during the day and then traveled northward at night when they were less likely to be caught. Since the Big Dipper points toward the North Star, the runaways could always be sure they were going in the right direction when they "followed the drinking gourd."

FOLLOW THE DRINKING GOURD

Traditional

When the sun comes— up and the first qua - il

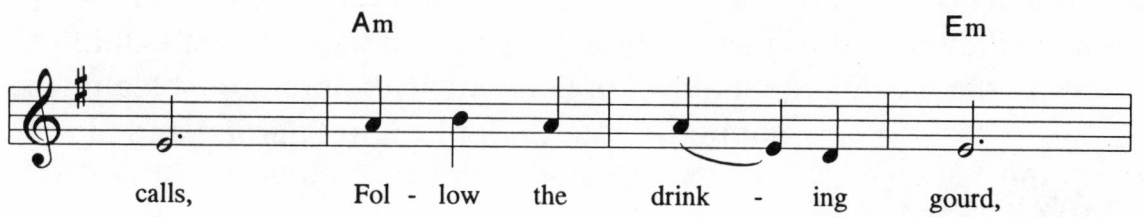

calls, Fol - low the drink - ing gourd,

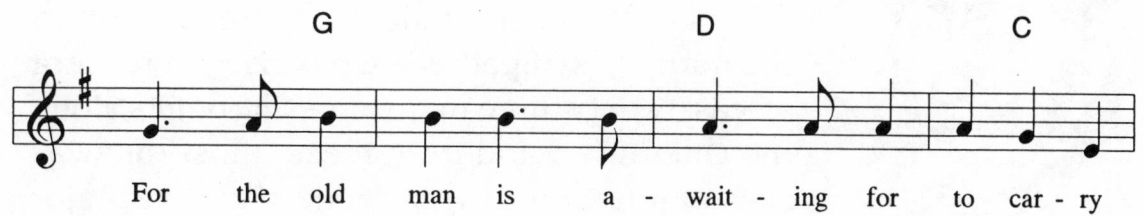

For the old man is a - wait - ing for to car - ry

you to free - dom, If you fol - low the drink - ing gourd.

CHORUS:

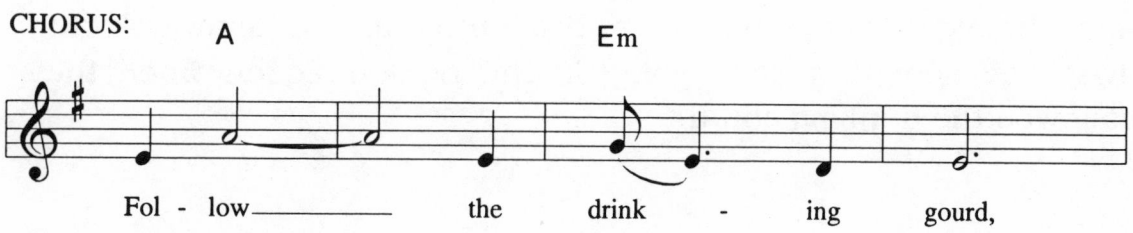

Fol - low——— the drink - ing gourd,

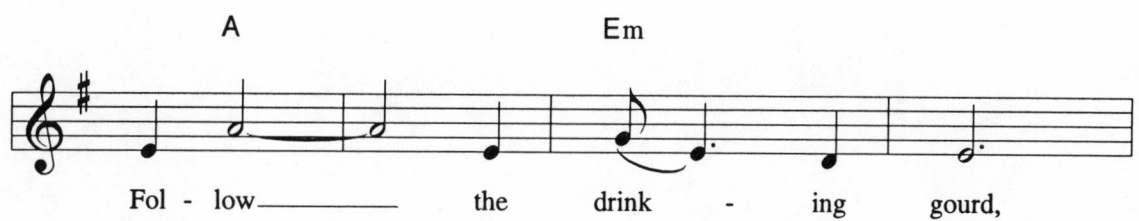

Fol - low——— the drink - ing gourd,

For the old man is a - wait - ing for to car - ry

you to free - dom, If you fol - low the drink - ing gourd.

Well the river bank makes a mighty good road;
The dead trees will show you the way.
On the left foot, peg foot, traveling on,
Follow the drinking gourd.
Chorus

The river ends between two hills,
Follow the drinking gourd.
There's another river on the other side,
If you follow the drinking gourd.
Chorus

Where the great big river meets the little river
Follow the drinking gourd.
For the old man is a-waiting for to carry you to freedom
If you follow the drinking gourd.
Chorus

Benjamin Hanby was born July 22, 1833, in Rushville, Ohio. He was the oldest son of Reverend William Hanby, a United Brethren minister, and his wife, Anne Miller. Reverend William Hanby was a staunch abolitionist, and his home was a station on the underground railroad. One incident from Benjamin Hanby's childhood that made a lasting impression on him was the arrival at the Hanby home of a runaway slave from Kentucky named Joseph Selby. Selby told the story of how his sweetheart had been sold away from Kentucky to Georgia. Brokenhearted, he had run away, hoping to reach Canada where he could find work and save enough money to buy his sweetheart's freedom. Selby was ill with pneumonia when he reached the Hanby home, and he died there, so his dream of reaching Canada was never accomplished. This incident occurred in 1842 when Benjamin Hanby was only nine years old, but it became the inspiration for his famous song "Darling Nelly Gray."

BENJAMIN HANBY

The Hanby family moved to Westerville, Ohio, in 1853, where Reverend William Hanby served as a United Brethren bishop and was a founder of Otterbein College, a small liberal arts college, which Benjamin Hanby attended. Benjamin Hanby wrote the song "Darling Nelly Gray" in 1856, when he was a sophomore at Otterbein.

After graduating from Otterbein in 1858, Benjamin Hanby worked briefly as a school principal and then as a minister. However, his real love was music. He founded a singing school in New Paris, Ohio, in 1864 and then took a position with Root & Cady music publishers in Chicago in 1866. During his life, Benjamin Hanby wrote over eighty songs and hymns, forty religious songs for children, and twenty inspirational songs. He died of tuberculosis in 1867.

"Darling Nelly Gray" is one of Benjamin Hanby's earliest and best known songs. It is a musical portrayal of the story Hanby heard in his youth of Joseph Selby and his sweetheart, Nelly Gray.

DARLING NELLY GRAY

Benjamin R. Hanby

There's a low green valley on the old Ken-tuck-y shore, Where I've whiled ma-ny hap-py hours a-way, A-sit-ting and a-sing-ing by the lit-tle cot-tage door, Where lived my dar-ling Nel-ly Gray.

CHORUS:

Oh, my poor Nel-ly Gray, They have tak-en you a-way, And I'll nev-er see my dar-ling an-y more; I'm

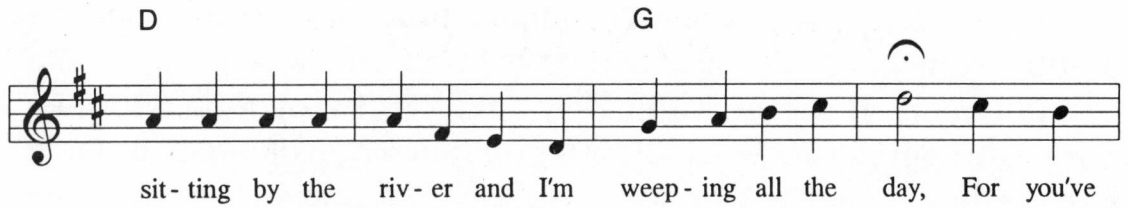

sit - ting by the riv - er and I'm weep - ing all the day, For you've

gone from the old Ken - tuck - y shore.

When the moon had climbed the mountain and the stars
    were shining, too,
Then I'd take my darling Nelly Gray,
And we'd float down the river in my little red canoe,
While my banjo sweetly I would play. *Chorus*

One night I went to see her, but "She's gone!" the neighbors say,
The white man bound her with his chain;
They have taken her to Georgia for to wear her life away,
As she toils in the cotton and the cane. *Chorus*

My canoe is under water and my banjo is unstrung,
I'm tired of living any more;
My eyes shall look downward and my song shall be unsung
While I stay on the old Kentucky shore. *Chorus*

My eyes are getting blinded and I cannot see my way;
Hark! there's somebody knocking at the door.
Oh, I hear the angels calling, and I see my Nelly Gray,
Farewell to the old Kentucky shore.

Chorus: Oh, my darling Nelly Gray, up in heaven there, they say,
That they'll never take you from me any more;
I'm a-coming, coming, coming, as the angels clear the way,
Farewell to the old Kentucky shore.

On April 12, 1861, when President Abraham Lincoln called for 75,000 volunteers at the onset of the Civil War, Ohio was given a quota of 13,000 men. However, within only a few weeks, over 30,000 men from Ohio had enlisted. Ohio men continued to volunteer in large numbers throughout the duration of the Civil War, and by the end of the war, 320,000 Ohioans had served in the Union army.

Many soldiers from Ohio were involved in the Battle of Stones River, fought near Murfreesboro, Tennessee, from December 31, 1862 to January 2, 1863. Union troops were victorious at the end of the three day battle, but there were extensive casualties on both sides.

The song "Stone River" is a ballad about a dying Union solder who was mortally wounded in this battle. It is often the case in the folk tradition that names of individuals or locations become blurred as a song is passed along orally. This song provides a good example. Although the river in Tennessee mentioned in the song is actually the Stones River, it became known as Stone River to Ohioans who sang about the Civil War battle which occurred along its banks.

STONE RIVER

Traditional

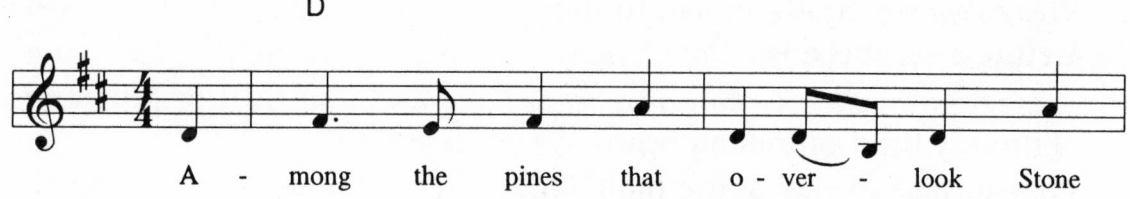

A - mong the pines that o - ver - look Stone

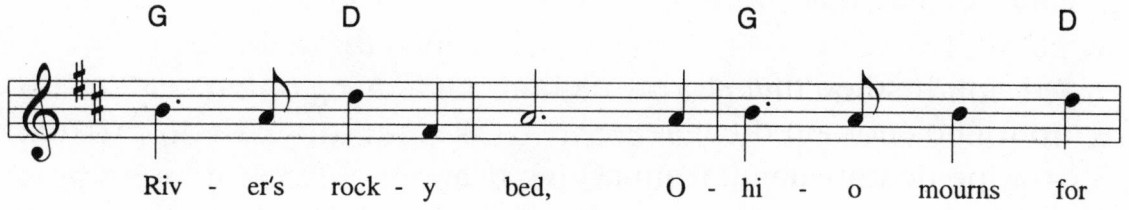

Riv - er's rock - y bed, O - hi - o mourns for

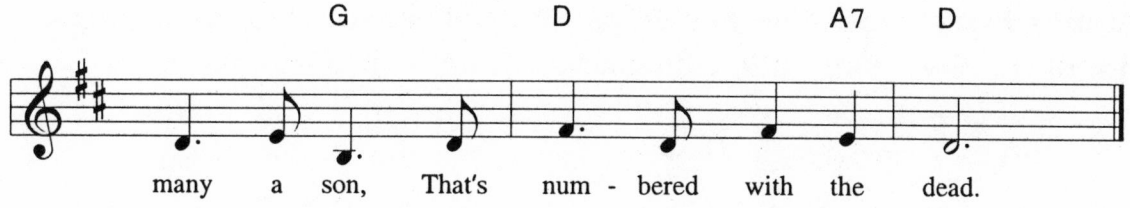

many a son, That's num - bered with the dead.

As night closed down the bloody scenes,
Returning o'er the dead,
I heard the pitiful moans of one
Laid low by mortal wounds.

I filled his canteen from a spring
Below Stone River's banks;
I built a fire of cedar wood,
The night being cold and damp.

They set me down to ask of him
If he did wish to send
Some last request of parting words
To a mother, sister, or friend.

"Tell sister that I've read with care
The holy ties in dear,
The Bible my mother gave to me
Before I volunteered."

"I'm very tired of talking now,
Please raise me up some high,
And fold my blankets close around,
And build a larger fire."

But, oh, he died that stormy night,
No friends nor kin drew near,
To wipe death's damp from off his brow,
Or shed an affectionate tear.

General John Hunt Morgan led a Confederate cavalry of 2,460 men which terrorized southern Indiana and Ohio during the summer of 1863. On July 9, they initially crossed the Ohio River from Kentucky into southern Indiana and then moved into Ohio a few miles north of Cincinnati. The cavalry, popularly known as "Morgan's Raiders," traveled east across southern Ohio avoiding cities and towns but looting and plundering in the countryside. On July 19, they attempted to recross the Ohio River at a ford opposite Buffington Island in Meigs County. However, Union troops and the Ohio militia caught up with them, and a brief battle took place.

About half of Morgan's troops were captured, but Morgan himself and the rest of his cavalry escaped and continued to move northward, looking for another place to cross the river. They found another ford about twenty miles north of Buffington Island, but only three hundred men had crossed when Union gunboats began to fire upon them. Morgan and the remainder of his forces continued to flee to the north. They were finally captured by Union troops and Ohio militiamen on July 26, 1863, at Salineville in Columbiana County.

GENERAL JOHN MORGAN

John Morgan was subsequently imprisoned in the Ohio state penitentiary in Columbus. He was not a prisoner for long, however. He and six of his officers escaped from the prison on November 27, 1863, and made their way back to the South. John Morgan continued to lead Confederate armies until he was killed in battle in 1864.

Morgan's Raid was the only Civil War action that took place on Ohio soil. The song "How Are You, John Morgan?" tells of Morgan's capture, imprisonment, and escape.

HOW ARE YOU, JOHN MORGAN?

Anonymous

"Here's Your Mule" (C. D. Benson)

A fa - mous re - bel once—— was caught, with

sa - ber bright—— in hand, Up - on—— a mule he

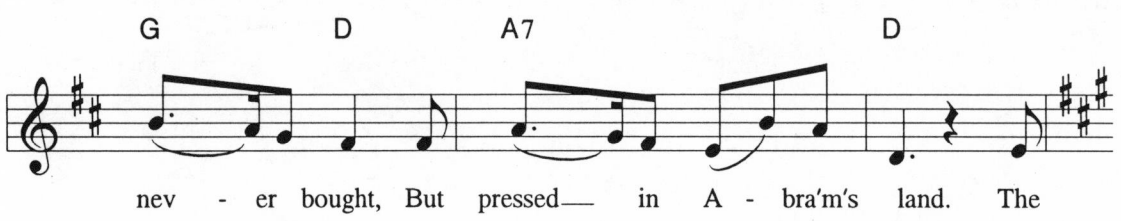

nev - er bought, But pressed—— in A - bra'm's land. The

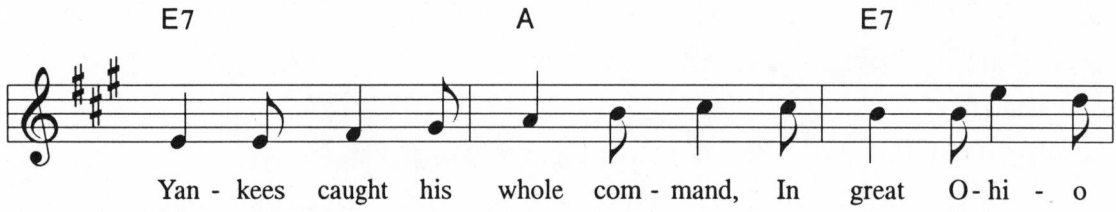

Yan - kees caught his whole com - mand, In great O - hi - o

state; And kept the lead - er of the band, To

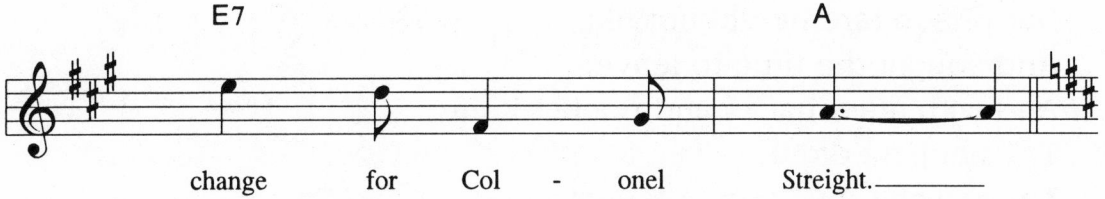

change   for   Col - onel   Streight.____

CHORUS:

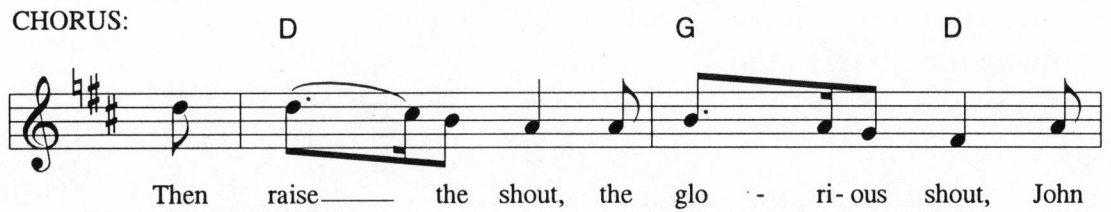

Then raise____ the shout, the glo - ri - ous shout, John

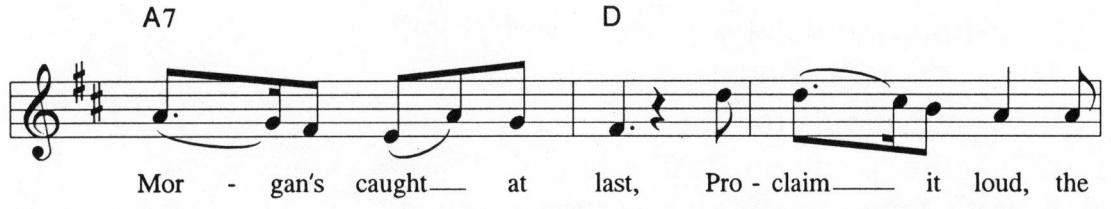

Mor - gan's caught____ at last, Pro - claim____ it loud, the

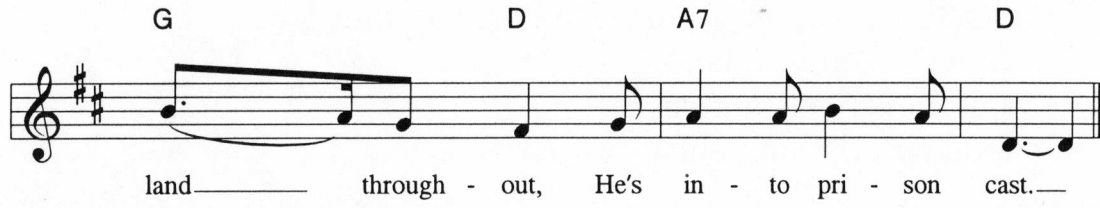

land____ through - out, He's in - to pri - son cast.____

A felon's cell was then prepared,
At David Tod's request,
And in Columbus prison shared
The convict's shaven crest.
And thus the Rebel chieftain's pride,
They sought to humble low,
But Southern valor won't subside
Nor less in prisons grow.
Chorus

But prison fare he did not like,
And sought the time to leave,
And with greenbacks and pocket knife,
The keepers did deceive.
They say he dug a tunnel 'neath
Its grated walls so grand,
And from the North he took "French leave"
Away for Dixie's land.
Chorus

John Morgan's gone like lightning flies,
Through every state and town;
Keep watch, and for the famous prize,
Five thousand dollars down.
But he is gone, too late, too late,
His whereabouts to find,
He's gone to call on Master Jeff,
Way down in Richmond town.

Final Chorus: Upon his mule, he's gone, they say,
To Dixie's promised land,
And at no very distant day
To lead a new command.

The economy of Ohio was almost completely based upon agriculture until 1850. From that time onward, however, it gradually began to change. The increased use of machinery and advances in transportation, such as the advent of the railroads, contributed to this change. By 1880, manufacturing had surpassed farming as the main focus of the economy of the state.

During the period from 1850 to 1880, the mining of iron ore in the Lake Superior area provided the raw material for many of Ohio's burgeoning industries. This iron ore was loaded into large ore boats and transported south through the Great Lakes to various ports, including Cleveland. The song "Red Iron Ore" describes one such voyage from Chicago to Escanaba, Michigan, where the iron ore was loaded, and was then sent on to the final destination of Cleveland.

RED IRON ORE

Traditional

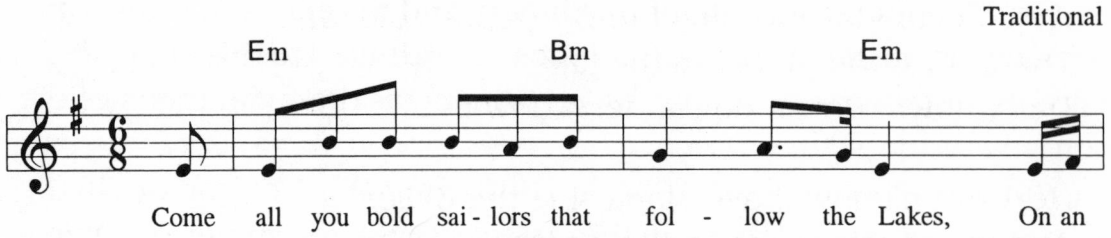

Come all you bold sai - lors that fol - low the Lakes, On an

i - ron ore ves - sel your liv - ing to make. I

shipped in Chi - ca - go, bid a - dieu to the shore, Bound a -

way to Es - ca - na - ba for red i - ron ore. Der - ry

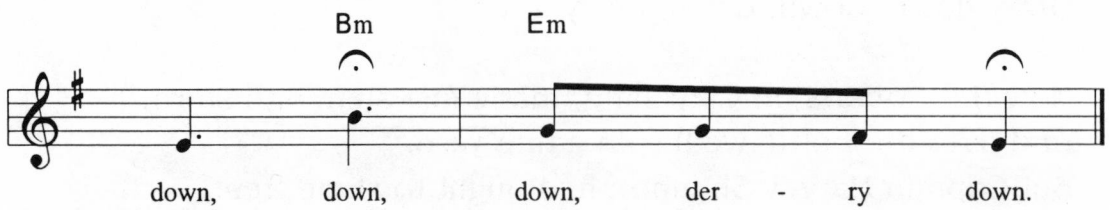

down, down, down, der - ry down.

In the month of September, the seventeenth day,
Two dollars and a quarter is all they would pay,
And on Monday morning the *Bridgeport* did take
The *E. C. Roberts* out in the lake.
Derry down, down, down, derry down.

Next morning we hove along side the *Exile*,
And soon were made fast to an iron-ore pile,
They lowered their chutes and like thunder did roar,
They spouted into us that red iron ore.
Derry down, down, down, derry down.

Some sailors took shovels and others took spades,
Some took wheelbarrows—each man to his trade,
We looked like red devils; our fingers got sore,
We cursed Escanaba and that red iron ore.
Derry down, down, down, derry down.

Across Saginaw Bay the *Roberts* did ride
With dark and deep water rolling over her side.
And now for Port Huron the *Roberts* must go,
Where the tug *Kate Williams* took us in tow.
Derry down, down, down, derry down.

We went though North Passage—Oh, Lord, how it blew!
And all 'round the Dummy a large fleet came, too.
The night being dark, Old Nick it would scare.
We hove up next morning and for Cleveland did steer.
Derry down, down, down, derry down.

Now the *Roberts* in Cleveland, made fast stem and stern,
And over the bottle we'll spin a fine yarn.
But Captain Harvey Shannon had ought to stand treat,
For getting to Cleveland ahead of the fleet.
Derry down, down, down, derry down.

Ohio has a rich and varied topography. The eastern half of the state is characterized by wooded, rolling hills, while the western part and the northern area along Lake Erie are primarily flat. Most of the state was originally covered with thick forests made up of such tree species as oak, maple, beech, hickory, walnut, and elm.

The original settlers of Ohio came from several different areas including Pennsylvania, Virginia, Kentucky, and New England. In addition, large numbers of Irish, Scotch-Irish, and Germans settled in the state. These groups, along with later immigrants of a wide variety of nationalities, merged and mingled to create the character of the modern Ohioan. Ohioans have a rich heritage of which they should be justly proud.

During the twentieth century, Ohio has grown into a predominantly industrial and commercial, rather than agricultural, state although Ohio's fertile farmland continues to produce abundant crops of corn, soybeans, and wheat. "The Hills of Ohio" was written by Alexander Auld, a nineteenth century singing school teacher, who was inspired by the beauty he saw all around him in Ohio.

THE HILLS OF OHIO

Alexander Auld

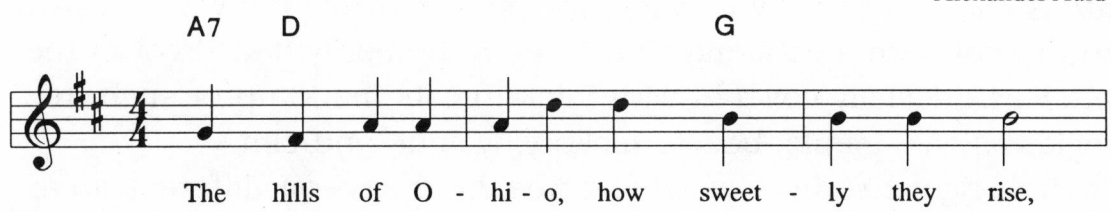

The hills of O - hi - o, how sweet - ly they rise,

In beau - ty of na - ture to blend with the skies;

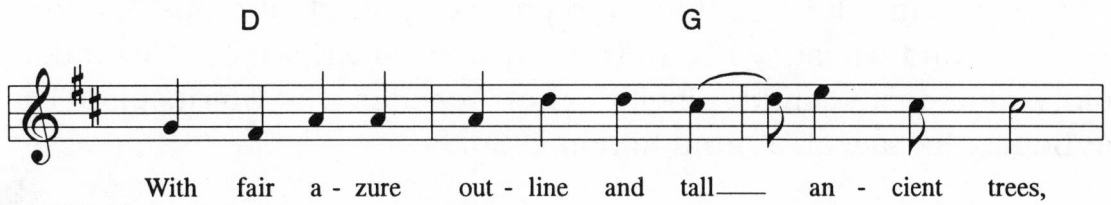

With fair a - zure out - line and tall__ an - cient trees,

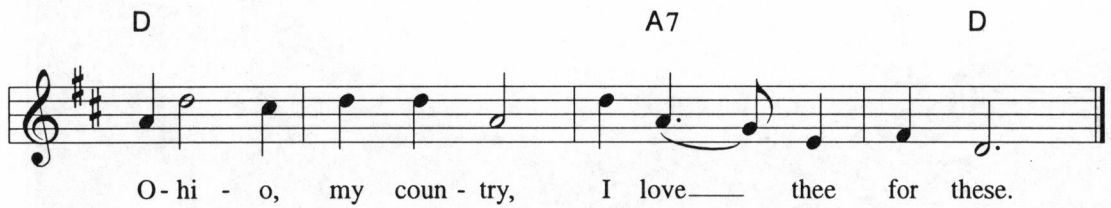

O - hi - o, my coun - try, I love__ thee for these.

The homes of Ohio, free, fortuned, and fair,
Full many hearts treasure a sister's love there;
E'en more than thy hill-sides or steamlets they please,
Ohio, my country, I love thee for these.

God shield thee, Ohio, dear land of my birth,
And thy children that wander afar o'er the earth;
My country thou art, where'er my lot's cast,
Take thou to thy bosom my ashes at last.

Appendix A
Guitar and Dulcimer Chords

Guitar Chords

The vertical lines represent the strings. The horizontal lines represent the frets.

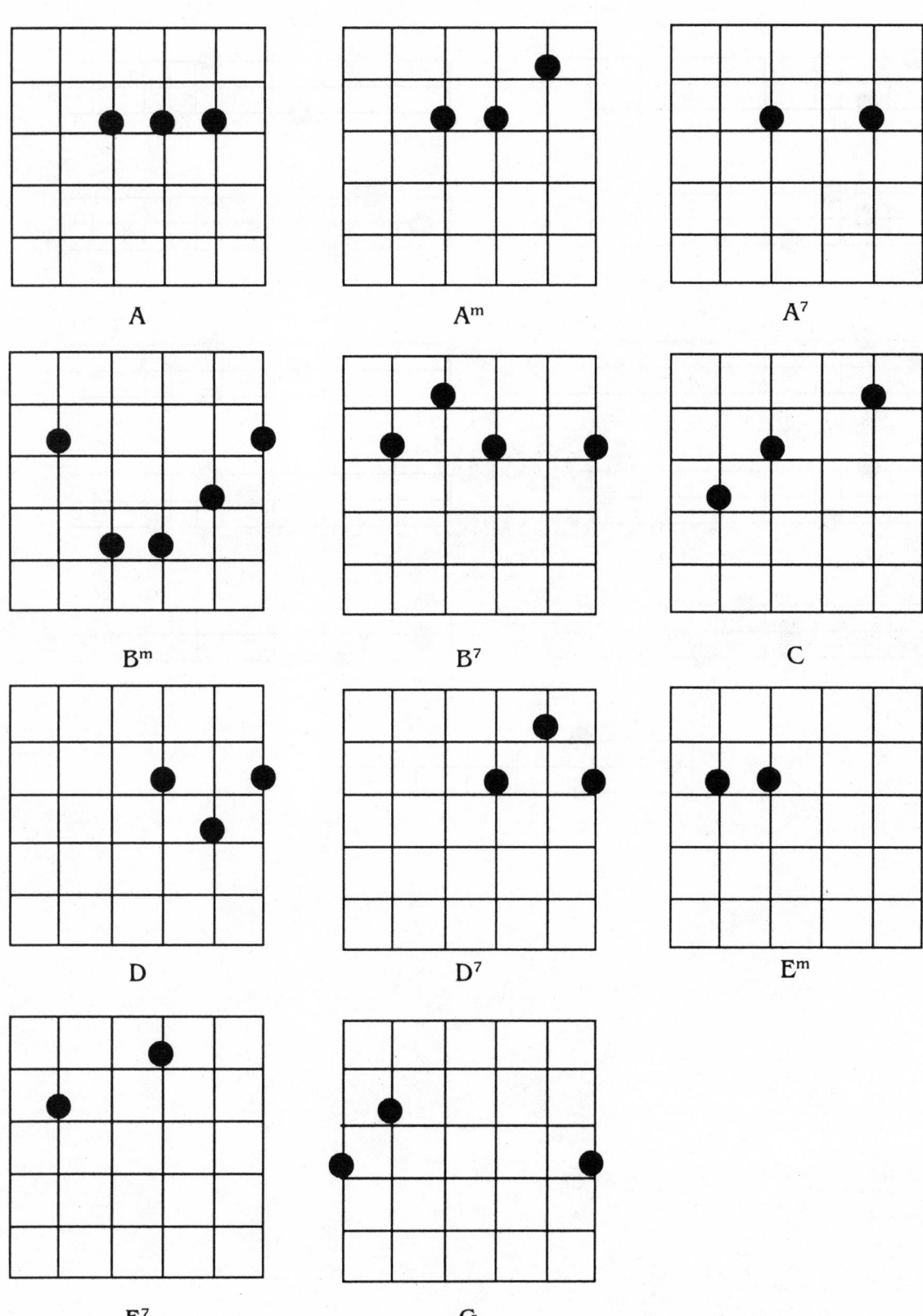

Dulcimer Chords

D A A Tuning

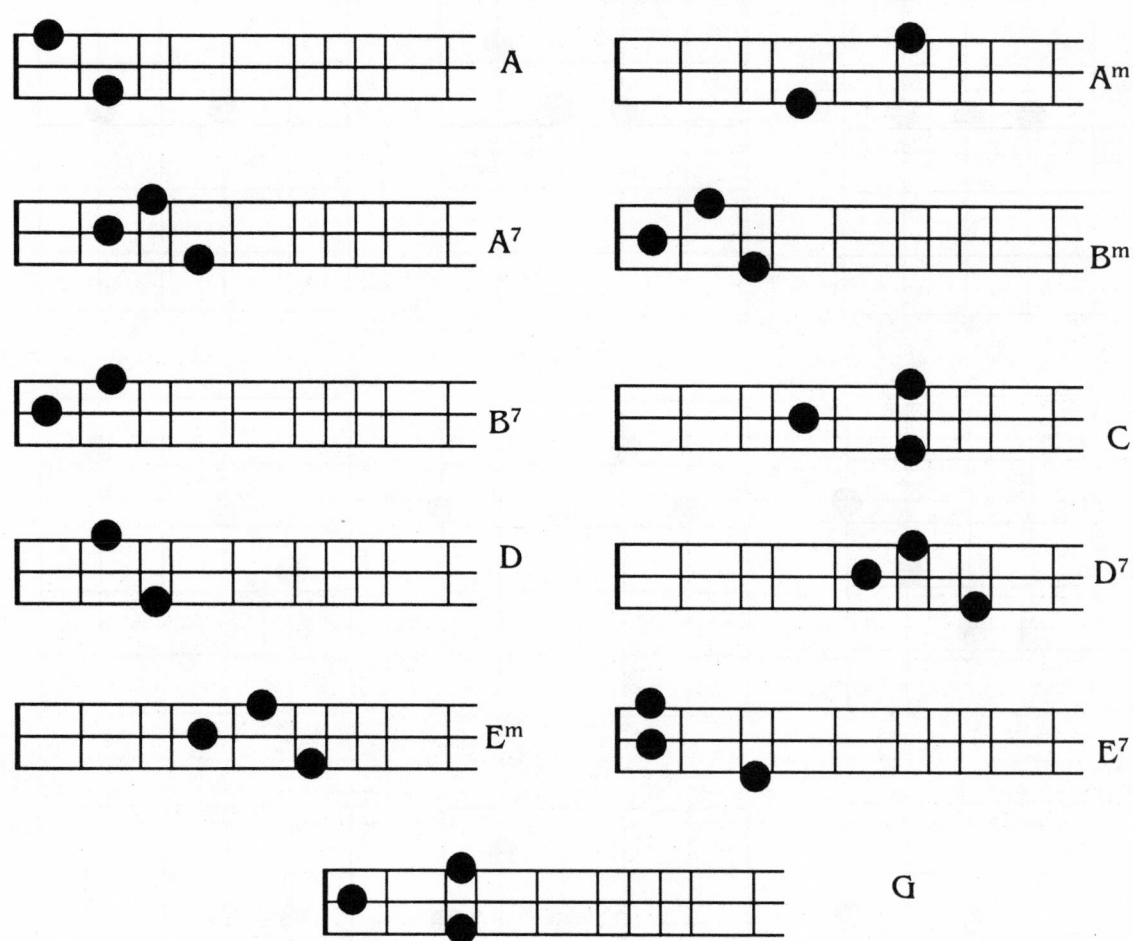

Dulcimer Chords

D A D Tuning

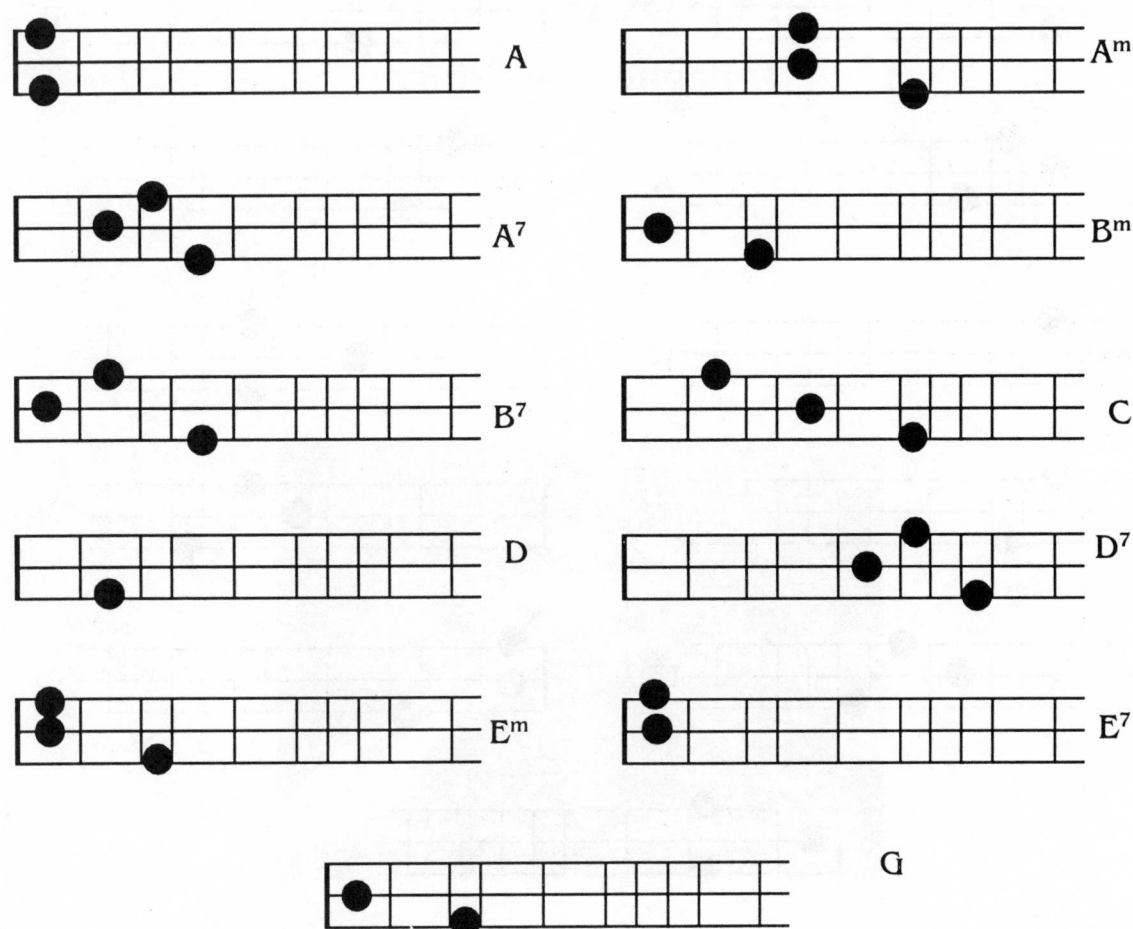

Appendix B
Dulcimer Tablature

On capoed tunes, frets are counted from the nut,
but the capoed fret is the open or zero fret.

C'EST L'AVIRON QUI NOUS MENE EN HAUT

DAA

5 5 4 3 7 7 7 7 7 7 8 7

5 5 4 3 7 7 7 7 7 7 8 7

7 7 8 10 8 7 8 7 6 5 4

CHORUS:

3 3 4 5 4 3 4 3 4 5 6 4

3 3 4 5 4 3 2 4 3

PETIT ROCHER DE LA HAUTE MONTAGNE

DAA
Capo at 1st Fret

6 7   8 8   7 6   7   8 8   7 6   5 4

6 7   8 8   7 6   7   8 8   7 6   5 4

6 6   7 6   6 7   7 7   5   6 5

4 6   8 8   7 6   5 6   5 4   3   4

LOGAN'S LAMENT

DAA

3   5   5 4   3 3   3   6   6 6

5   5 5   5 4 3   7 7   8 8   8

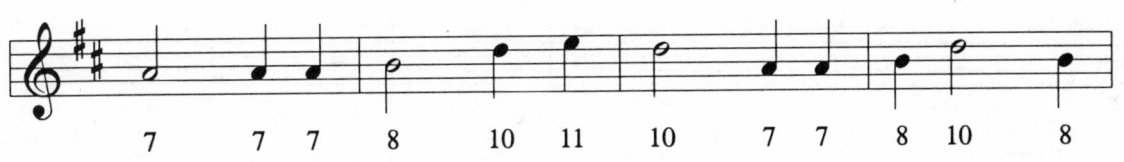

7   7 7   8   10 11   10   7 7   8 10   8

7   3 4   5   7 8   7   7 7   7 7   5

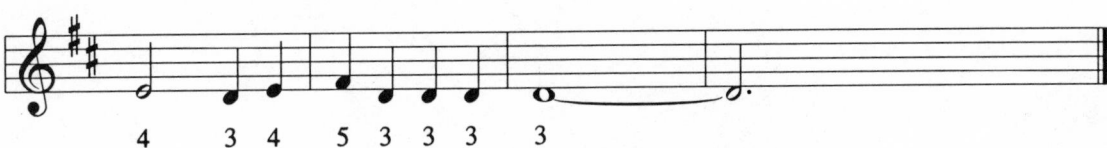

4 3 4   5 3 3 3   3

BATTLE OF POINT PLEASANT

DAA

5 5 6 7   8 7 8 7 5

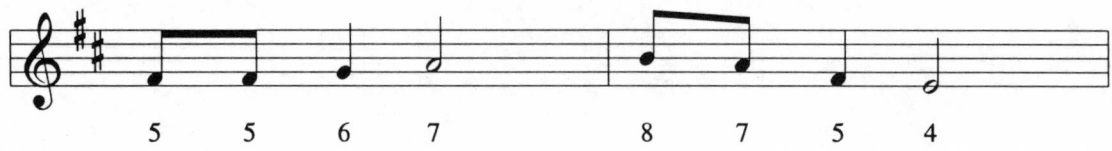

5 5 6 7   8 7 5 4

3 3 3 5   3 5 6 7 5

5 5 6 7   4 5 6 5 3

JESUS, HEAR OUR PRAYER

DAA

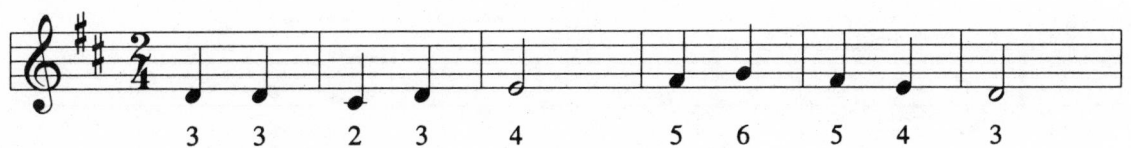

3 3 2 3 4 5 6 5 4 3

5 6 7 6 5 4 6 5 4 3 4

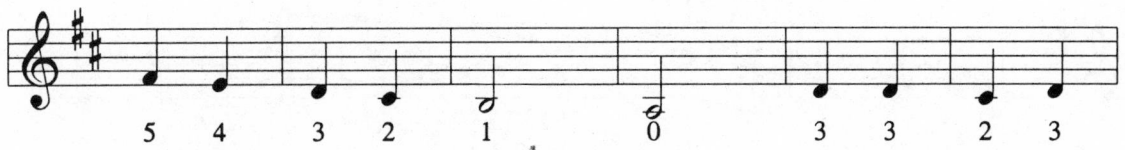

5 4 3 2 1 0 3 3 2 3

4 5 6 5 4 3

ST. CLAIR'S DEFEAT

DAA
Capo at 1st Fret

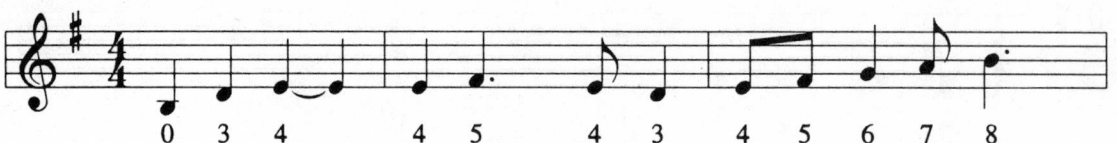

0   3   4   4   5   4   3   4   5   6   7   8

6   7   8   10   4   8   8   7   6   4   4   3   4

4   5   4   8   10   4   8   8   7   6   7   8   10   4

4   4   5   4   8   10   11   8   8   7   6   4   4

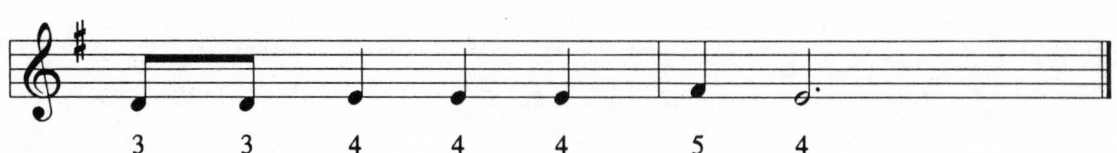

3   3   4   4   4   5   4

PLEASANT OHIO

DAA

3 4 5 5 5 5 5

7 7 5 5 4 4 5 4

7 7 8 7 8 9 10 3

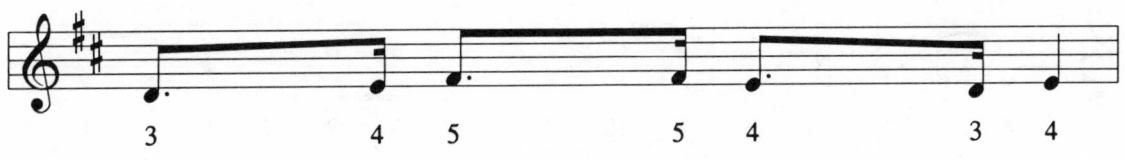

3 4 5 5 4 3 4

3 4 5 5 5 5 5

7 5 5 4 4 5 4

PERRY'S VICTORY

DAA
Capo at 3rd Fret

6   0   0   0   6   6   6   7   8   7   8   6   6

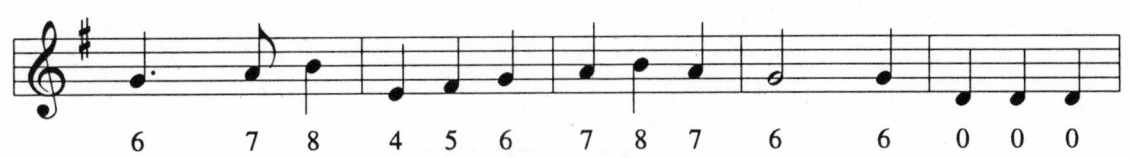

6   7   8   4   5   6   7   8   7   6   6   0   0   0

6   6   6   7   8   7   8   6   6   6   7   8   4   5   6

7   8   7   6   6   6   8   10   10   8   10   11   7   7

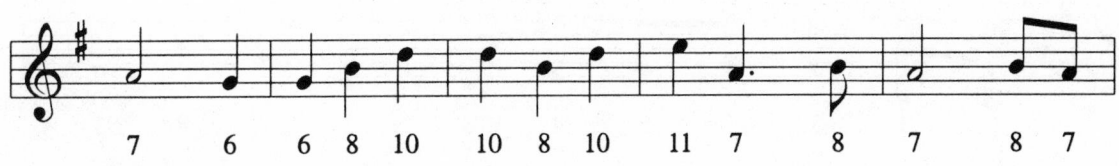

7   6   6   8   10   10   8   10   11   7   8   7   8   7

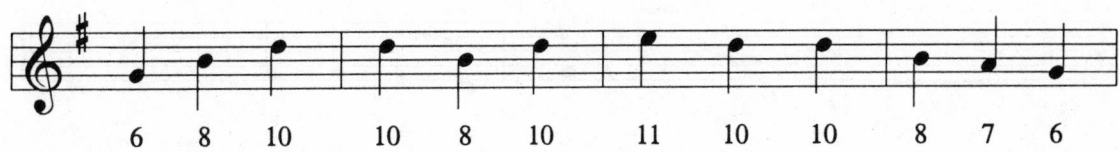

6   8   10   10   8   10   11   10   10   8   7   6

6 7 8   4 5 6   7 8 7   6

SHAWNEETOWN

DAA

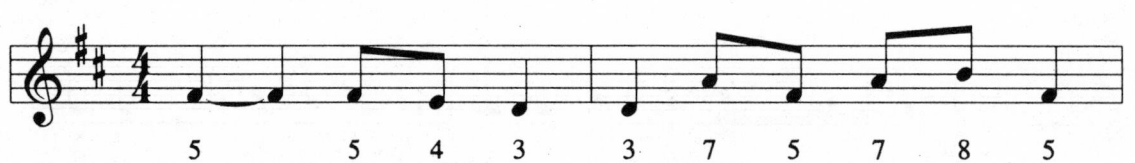

5   5 4 3   3 7 5 7 8 5

10 10 7 8 7 5   3 4 5 5   4 3

CHORUS:

0 1 5 5 5 4 3   3 7 8 5

10 10 7 8 7 5   3 4 5 5   4 3

NANCY TILL

DAA

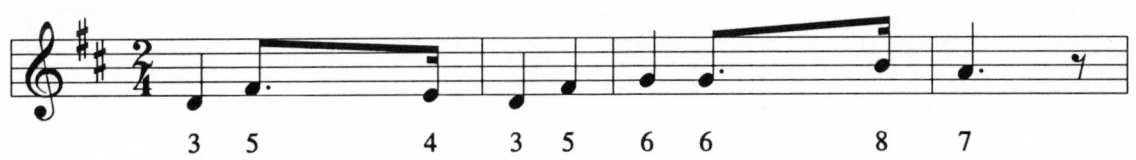

3 5 4 3 5 6 6 8 7

3 5 4 3 4 5 6 7 6 4 5 3 0

3 5 4 3 5 5 6 8 7 3

3 3 4 2 3 3 5 5 7 6 4 5 3

CHORUS:

7 7 10 5 8 6 4 5

6 5 6 7 8 2 2 3 5 7

7   7   10   10   5   7   8   7   6   4

5   6   7   8   2   4   3   3

ON THE BANKS OF THE OHIO

DAA

0 3 5 5 5 5 5 5 5 4 5 7

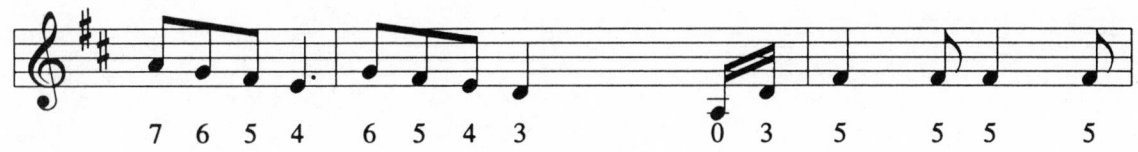

7 6 5 4 6 5 4 3 0 3 5 5 5 5

5 4 5 7 7 7 7 8 7 6 5 4 3

CHORUS:

0 3 5 5 5 5 5 5 5 4 5 7

7 4 7 5 7 7 0 3 5 5 5 5 5 5

5 4 5 7 7 7 6 2 3

THE OLD SKIPPER

DAA

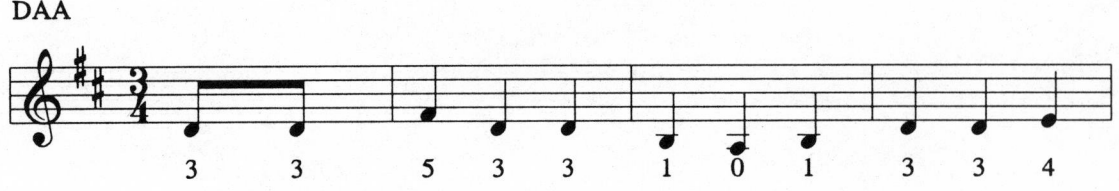

3 3 5 3 3 1 0 1 3 3 4

5 3 5 3 3 1 0 1 3 3 4

3 5 7 5 5 4 3 5 4 3 3

5 3 5 3 3 1 0 1 3 3 4 3

FAIRY PALACE

DAA

7 10 10 8 7 8 7 5 7

10 10 8 7 8 7 10 10 8 7

CHORUS:

8 8 10 10 5 5 5 3 4 3 4

5 5 5 4 4 3 3 3 3 3 10 10

8 7 8 10 10 10 8 7 5 3 4

5 5 4 4 3

116

THE MULES RAN OFF

DAA

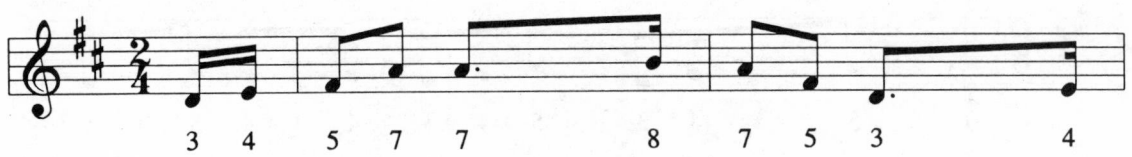

3 4   5 7 7   8   7 5 3   4

5 5 4 3   4   3 4 5 7 7   8

7 5 3   4   5 5 4 4   3

CHORUS:

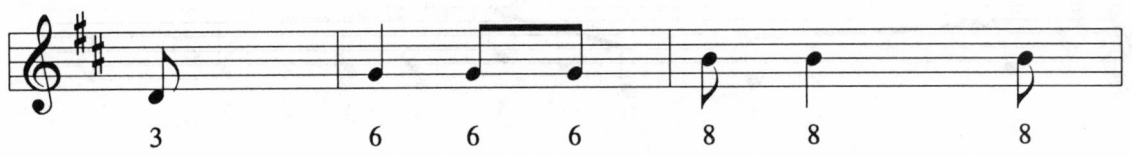

3   6 6 6   8 8   8

7 7 5 3   4   3 4 5 7 7   8

7 5 3   4   5 5 4 4   3

THAT OLD TOWPATH

DAA

5   4   3   5   4   3   4   3   4   5   3   3

3   2   1   0   3   5   4   3   4   3

CHORUS:

0   5   4   3   5   4   3   4   3   4   5   3   3

3   2   1   0   3   5   4   3   4   3

LAST TRIP IN THE FALL

DAA
Capo at 1st Fret

5   6 4 5 4 4 3 0 0   0 4 4 4 4   0

4   4 6 7 8 8 10 8   7 5 3 5 4   0

4   4 6 7 8 8 10 8   7 5 3 5 7   5

6 4 5 4 4 3 0 0   0 4 4 5 4

OLD TIPPECANOE

DAA

0 3 3 3 5 4 3 5 7 8

7 5 3 3 4 5 1 0 3 3 3

5 4 3 5 7 8 7 5 3 4 5 4

CHORUS:

3 7 7 5 7 7 8 9

10 8 7 5 3 3 4 5 1 0

3 3 3 5 4 3 5 7 8

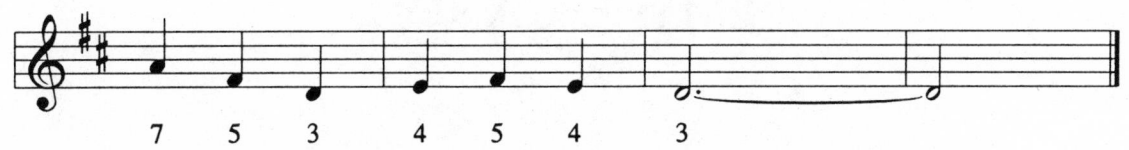

THE WYANDOTTE FAREWELL SONG

DAA

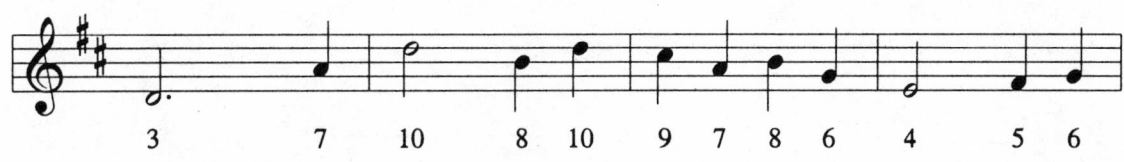

SIMPLE GIFTS

DAA

CHORUS:

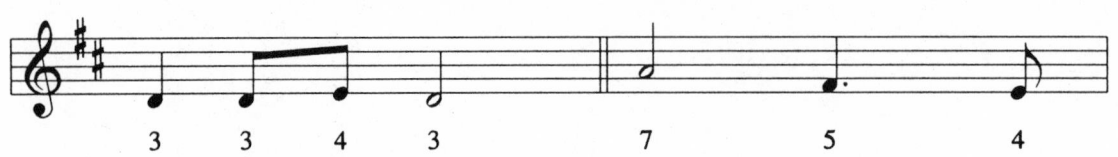

FOLLOW THE DRINKING GOURD

DAA
Capo at 1st Fret

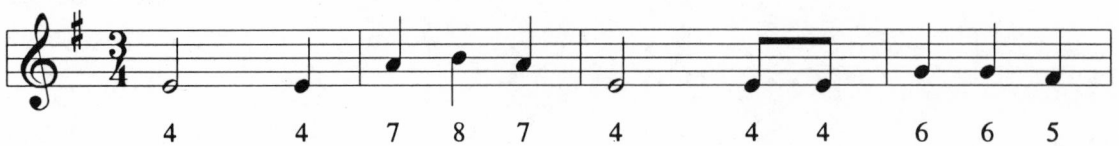

4   4 7 8 7 4   4 4 6 6 5

4   7 8 7 7 4 3 4

6 7 8 8 8 8 7 7 7 7 6 4

6 6 5 5 5 5 6 4 4 3 0 3 4

CHORUS:

4 7   4 6 4 3 4

4 7   4 6 4 3 4

6 7 8 8 8 8 7 7 7 7 6 4

6 6 5 5 5 5 6 4 4 3 0 3 4

DARLING NELLY GRAY

DAA

5 6 7 7 8 7 5 4 3 6 7 8 9

10 9 8 7 7 7 8 7 5 3 4 5 6

7 7 7 7 7 5 4 3 6 7 8 9 10 9 8

7 7 7 7 7 5 4 3 6 7 8 9 10 9 8

5 5 6 7 7 7 7 8 7 5 3 4 5 6

7 7 7 7 7 5 4 3 6 7 8 9 10 9 8

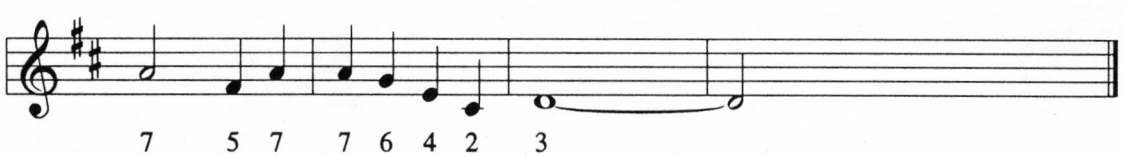

7 5 7 7 6 4 2 3

STONE RIVER

DAA

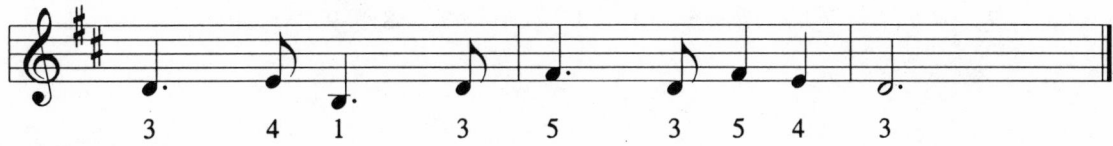

THE HILLS OF OHIO

DAA

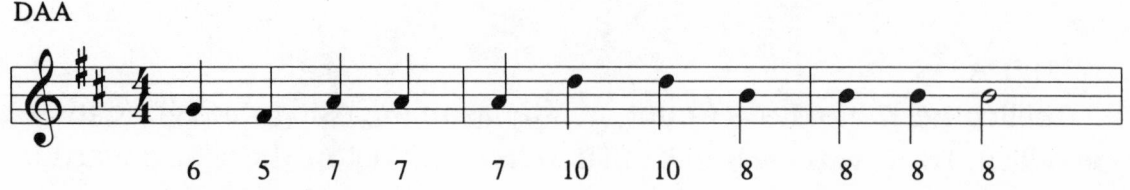

6 5 7 7 7 10 10 8 8 8 8

7 7 5 5 5 7 7 7 4 4 4

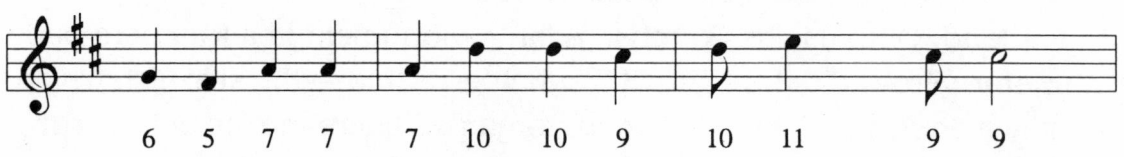

6 5 7 7 7 10 10 9 10 11 9 9

7 10 9 10 10 7 10 7 6 4 5 3

OHIO HISTORICAL SITES

ADENA

Chillicothe, Ohio (Ross County). Adena, an imposing sandstone mansion built in 1807, was the home of Thomas Worthington, the sixth governor of Ohio. The view from the hilltop site is said to have inspired the design of the Great Seal of the State of Ohio. Take Adena Road west off of S.R. 104.

AUGLAIZE VILLAGE

Defiance, Ohio (Defiance County). The village includes two small museums containing a variety of pioneer items and several restored buildings dating from the period 1860 to 1920. Take U.S. 24 two miles west of Defiance to Krouse Road. Turn left and go one-quarter of a mile.

BUFFINGTON ISLAND STATE MEMORIAL

Portland, Ohio (Meigs County). A large monument in a four acre park commemorates the only real Civil War battle in Ohio — the skirmish which took place on July 19, 1863, between Morgan's Raiders and the Union Army. Buffington Island State Memorial is located on S.R. 124 about twenty miles east of Pomeroy.

CAESAR CREEK PIONEER VILLAGE

Harveysburg, Ohio (Warren County). Original log cabins and other pioneer structures which were moved to the site from various parts of Warren County make up the village, which is located in Caesar Creek State Park. From S.R. 73 at Harveysburg, take Co. Rd. 12 about one mile south to Oregonia Road and turn right. Continue for about one mile and then turn right on Clarksville Road. This road ends near the village area. Signs along the route direct visitors to the pioneer village.

CAMPUS MARTIUS MUSEUM

Marietta, Ohio (Washington County). The museum provides exhibits on pioneer life in the Northwest Territory and includes the Rufus Putnam house, which dates from 1788 and is the oldest surviving log cabin in the state. The museum is located at the corner of Washington and Second streets in Marietta.

CARRIAGE HILL

Dayton, Ohio (Montgomery County). Carriage Hill is a restored nineteenth century farmstead. The farm was established in 1830 by Daniel Arnold and was worked by members of the Arnold family until 1910. To reach Carriage Hill, exit I-70 at S.R. 201 and go a short distance north to Shull Road. Turn right and proceed to the farm at 7860 Shull Road.

CENTURY VILLAGE

Burton, Ohio (Geauga County). The village consists of a number of restored buildings which depict nineteenth century life in a typical town in the Western Reserve area of northeastern Ohio. (The Western Reserve was an area of northeastern Ohio that was set aside for settlers moving west from Connecticut after the Revolutionary War.) Century Village is located at the junction of S.R. 87 and S.R. 700 at the south end of the town square in Burton.

CLIFTON MILL

Clifton, Ohio (Greene County). Clifton Mill was established on the Little Miami River in 1803. It burned to the ground in the 1840's, but was rebuilt in 1869. The mill, which is still in operation, is located at the south end of the village of Clifton.

FALLEN TIMBERS MEMORIAL

Maumee, Ohio (Lucas County). The ten-acre site was the location of the Battle of Fallen Timbers. General Anthony Wayne and his army defeated a large group of Indians at this spot on August 20, 1794. This decisive battle led to the signing of the Treaty of Green Ville in 1795. To reach the site, leave U.S. 24 at the first exit south of I-475. Turn south and follow the signs for about one mile.

FLINT RIDGE

Brownsville, Ohio (Licking County). Flint Ridge is the site of a major pre-historic flint quarry, which was used extensively by Ohio's Indians. A small museum is present at the site, and trails through the woods pass several quarry pits. Flint Ridge is three miles north of Brownsville on Co. Rd. 668.

FORT ANCIENT STATE MEMORIAL

Southeast of Lebanon, Ohio (Warren County). This park includes a large

Hopewell Indian hilltop earthwork on a bluff overlooking the Little Miami River. A small museum is present at the site. Fort Ancient is located seven miles southeast of Lebanon on S.R. 350.

FORT DEFIANCE MEMORIAL

Defiance, Ohio (Defiance County). This is the site of Fort Defiance, which was built at the confluence of the Maumee and Auglaize Rivers in 1794 by General Anthony Wayne. From here, he marched north to defeat the Indians at the Battle of Fallen Timbers. Two cannons are the only remaining evidence of the fort. The Fort Defiance Memorial is located at the end of Washington Avenue in the town of Defiance.

FORT HILL STATE MEMORIAL

North of Sinking Spring, Ohio (Highland County). Fort Hill preserves a large Hopewell period hilltop earthwork overlooking Brush Creek. A small museum is present at the site. Fort Hill is five miles north of Sinking Spring. Take S.R. 41 north to Twp. Rd. 256. Turn left and go about a mile.

FORT JEFFERSON

Fort Jefferson, Ohio (Darke County). This is the site of one of the forts built by General Arthur St. Clair during his campaign against the Indians in 1791. Fort Jefferson is located at the junction of Co. Rd. 24 and S.R. 121 in Darke County.

FORT LAURENS

Bolivar, Ohio (Tuscarawas County). This is the site of the earliest colonial fort in Ohio. It was built by General Lachlan McIntosh in 1778. The fort withstood an Indian attack in February 1779, but it was then abandoned in the summer of that year, and the garrison withdrew to Fort Pitt (now Pittsburgh) because the fort proved to be too difficult to resupply. A small museum provides interpretive displays. Fort Laurens is located on Co. Rd. 102 at the south edge of the town of Bolivar.

FORT MEIGS

Perrysburg, Ohio (Wood County). Fort Meigs was built in 1813 on the orders of William Henry Harrison in order to protect Ohio and Indiana from invasion by the British during the War of 1812. It withstood two attacks by the British and Indians in May and July of 1813. A reconstruction of the fort

can be found at the site. Fort Meigs is located on S.R. 65 (West River Road) in Perrysburg.

FORT RECOVERY STATE MEMORIAL
Fort Recovery, Ohio (Mercer County). Fort Recovery stands at the site of the battle in which General Arthur St. Clair was badly defeated by the Indians in 1791. General Anthony Wayne ordered a fort built at the site of St. Clair's defeat in late 1793, and another battle, which the American army won, took place there on June 30, 1794. A small museum, a monument, and two reconstructed blockhouses connected by a stockade can be found at present-day Fort Recovery. The site is located near the junction of S.R. 119 and S.R. 49 in the town of Fort Recovery.

FORT ST. CLAIR
Eaton, Ohio (Preble County). This is the site of one of the forts built by Arthur St. Clair's army in 1791. Nothing remains of the fort, but its four corners are marked by stones. Take S.R. 122 west out of Eaton and turn left on S.R. 355.

GNADENHUTTEN MONUMENT
Gnadenhutten, Ohio (Tuscarawas County). A large monument marks the location of the massacre of ninety-six Christian Delaware Indians, who were ruthlessly murdered by a frontier militia in 1782. A small museum is also present at the site. The park is located one mile south of the center of Gnadenhutten. To reach the park, follow the historic signs.

GOVERNOR BEBB PRESERVE
West of Hamilton, Ohio (Butler County). A number of early log cabins and a log tavern from various parts of southwestern Ohio have been moved to this site to create an Ohio village of the year 1812. One of the cabins was the birthplace of William Bebb, who was governor of Ohio from 1846 to 1848. Take S.R. 129 west from Hamilton for about fourteen miles. Turn left on Co. Rd. 209 and go a little over a mile. Turn right on S.R. 126 . The preserve entrance will be on the left in less than a mile.

HALE FARM AND VILLAGE
Bath, Ohio (Summit County). The village provides an example of a Western Reserve area town of the early nineteenth century. Across the road,

Hale Farm is a typical example of a mid-nineteenth century farmstead. The complex is located in the Cuyahoga Valley National Recreation Area at 2686 Oak Hill Road near Bath.

HANBY HOUSE

Westerville, Ohio (Franklin County). This was the family home of nineteenth century songwriter Benjamin Hanby. The Hanby family lived here from 1853 to 1870, and their home served as a stop on the Underground Railroad. Hanby House is located at 160 W. Main Street in Westerville.

HARRISON TOMB

North Bend, Ohio (Hamilton County). A monument and the tomb of William Henry Harrison, ninth president of the United States, can be found at the site. It is located west of S.R. 50 off Cliff Road.

HISTORIC LYME VILLAGE

Bellevue, Ohio (Huron County). A number of restored buildings dating from the early to middle nineteenth century make up this example of a typical northern Ohio village. Historic Lyme Village is located two miles east of Bellevue on S.R. 113, just west of S.R. 4.

INDIAN MILL

Upper Sandusky, Ohio (Wyandot County). This was the location of a mill that was built by the federal government in 1820 for the local Wyandot Indians. It was used until the Wyandots were forced to leave Ohio in 1843. The present mill at the site dates from 1861. The mill is no longer operational because the water level in the Sandusky River has dropped since the nineteenth century. Indian Mill is located three miles northeast of Upper Sandusky along Co. Rd. 47.

INSCRIPTION ROCK

Kelleys Island, Ohio (Erie County). Prehistoric pictographs showing human and animal figures cover the surface of a large limestone boulder. Inscription Rock is located on the south shore of Kelleys Island.

LEO PETROGLYPH

Leo, Ohio (Jackson County). Prehistoric Indian carvings of humans and

animals can be seen on the surface of a large, flat sandstone boulder. Leo Petroglyph is located five miles northwest of Jackson. Take Co. Rd. 28 off of U.S. 35 to the village of Leo. From there, turn left on Twp. Rd. 224.

LOCKINGTON LOCKS

Lockington, Ohio (Shelby County). A series of well preserved locks from the Miami and Erie Canal can be seen. The locks are located near the south edge of the village of Lockington.

LOGAN ELM MEMORIAL

South of Circleville, Ohio (Pickaway County). A number of monuments are present at the site where Chief Logan of the Mingo tribe is thought to have made his famous speech in 1774. The elm tree, under which the speech was said to have been given, died in 1965, but a plaque marks its former location. Logan Elm Memorial is located five miles south of Circleville. It is one mile east of U.S. 23 on S.R. 361.

MIAMISBURG MOUND

Miamisburg, Ohio (Montgomery County). This Adena-period burial mound is the tallest conical mound in Ohio. It is located on Mound Avenue one mile south of S.R. 725.

MOUND CITY GROUP NATIONAL MONUMENT

Chillicothe, Ohio (Ross County). This thirteen acre park contains twenty-three prehistoric Hopewell burial mounds encircled by a low earthwork. A small museum is located at the site. Mound City Group is located on S.R. 104 about three miles north of Chillicothe.

MOUNDBUILDERS STATE MEMORIAL

Newark, Ohio (Licking County). A large circular earthwork surrounds three low Hopewell burial mounds. A small museum is also located here. Moundbuilders State Memorial is located on S.R. 79 on the south side of Newark.

OHIO HISTORICAL CENTER

Columbus, Ohio (Franklin County). This large museum houses extensive exhibits on Ohio's natural history, archaeology, and history. It is located at the Seventeenth Avenue exit from I-71 on the north side of Columbus.

OHIO RIVER MUSEUM

Marietta, Ohio (Washington County). This museum contains exhibits on the history of the Ohio River including the development of transportation on the river and the steamboat era. The *W. P. Snyder Jr.*, a steam-powered, sternwheeled towboat, is moored in the river outside the museum and can also be toured. The Ohio River Museum is located at the intersection of Front and St. Clair streets in Marietta.

OHIO VILLAGE

Columbus, Ohio (Franklin County). Ohio Village is a reconstructed Ohio county seat of the mid-nineteenth century. It is located at the Seventeenth Avenue exit from I-71 on the north side of Columbus adjacent to the Ohio Historical Center.

OUR HOUSE

Gallipolis, Ohio (Gallia County). Our House is a three-story brick river tavern which was built in 1819. It is located on First Street between Locust and State streets in downtown Gallipolis.

PERRY'S VICTORY AND INTERNATIONAL PEACE MEMORIAL

Put-in-Bay, Ohio (Ottawa County). A three hundred fifty-two foot high granite pillar commemorates Oliver Hazard Perry's victory in the Battle of Lake Erie on September 10, 1813. An elevator takes visitors to the top of the memorial for a panoramic view of the Lake Erie islands. The monument is located in the village of Put-in-Bay on South Bass Island.

PIQUA HISTORICAL AREA

Piqua, Ohio (Miami County). The Piqua Historical Area includes the Historic Indian Museum; the farm of John Johnston, who was a federal Indian agent in western Ohio from 1812 to 1830; and a restored section of the Miami and Erie Canal, where visitors can ride in a reconstructed canalboat. Take S.R. 66 northwest from Piqua and turn right on Hardin Road.

RANKIN HOUSE

Ripley, Ohio (Brown County). The home of John Rankin, a Presbyterian minister and abolitionist, was an important stop on the Underground Railroad. It is estimated that John Rankin and his wife, Jean, may have aided

as many as two thousand runaway slaves between the years 1825 and 1865. Rankin House is located on a hill overlooking the Ohio River and the town of Ripley. It can be reached by taking Race Street off of S.R. 52.

ROSCOE VILLAGE

Coshocton, Ohio (Coshocton County). Roscoe Village was an important commercial town along the Ohio and Erie Canal during the mid-nineteenth century. The buildings of Roscoe Village are mostly original and have been restored to their nineteenth century appearance. A section of the canal has also been restored, and visitors can take rides on the canalboat *Monticello III*. Roscoe Village is on Whitewoman Street near the junction of S.R. 16 and S.R. 83 at the edge of Coshocton.

SAUDER FARM AND CRAFT VILLAGE

Archbold, Ohio (Fulton County). The village is made up of restored nineteenth century town and farm buildings. It is located one and three-quarters miles northeast of Archbold on S.R. 2.

SCHOENBRUNN VILLAGE

New Philadelphia, Ohio (Tuscarawas County). Schoenbrunn was founded in 1772 by David Zeisberger and John Heckewelder, Moravian missionaries to the Delaware Indians. However, the missionaries and their Delaware converts were forced to abandon the village during the Revolutionary War. Schoenbrunn has been reconstructed and consists of a number of log buildings. The original cemetery is still extant. Schoenbrunn is located on S.R. 259 at the southeastern edge of New Philadelphia.

SERPENT MOUND

Northwest of Locust Grove, Ohio (Adams County). Serpent Mound is a large prehistoric effigy mound in the shape of a snake. Several Adena burial mounds and a small museum are also present at the site. Serpent Mound is located four miles northwest of Locust Grove on S.R. 73.

SLATE RUN LIVING HISTORICAL FARM

Northeast of Ashville, Ohio (Pickaway County). Slate Run Living Historical Farm is a working farm depicting 1880's farm life in central Ohio. To reach Slate Run Farm from U.S. 23 turn east on S.R. 752. Take S.R. 752 to S.R. 674 and turn left. Go two miles and turn left on Marcy Road. The

farm entrance is on the right after about a mile.

SUNWATCH

Dayton, Ohio (Montgomery County). SunWatch is a reconstructed twelfth century Fort Ancient Indian village located on an actual Fort Ancient village site. On-going archaeological excavations conducted by the Dayton Museum of Natural History can be observed during the summer months. Take exit 51 off I-75. Go west on Nicholas Road and turn left on West River Road. The site is located at 2301 West River Road.

ZOAR VILLAGE

Zoar, Ohio (Tuscarawas County). Zoar Village was founded by German immigrants as a communal settlement in 1817. The village prospered until the 1850's when a slow decline began. The communal experiment was ultimately disbanded in 1898. A number of restored buildings can be found in the village. Zoar Village is located on S.R. 212 in the town of Zoar.

Ohio History Bibliography

Abdy, Harry Bennett. *On the Ohio*. New York : Dodd, Mead, and Company, 1919.

Andrews, Edward D. *The Gift To Be Simple : Songs, Dances and Rituals of the American Shakers*. New York : Dover, 1962.

Banta, R. E. *The Ohio*. New York : Rinehart and Company, 1949.

Berton, Pierre. *Flames Across the Border: The Canadian-American Tragedy, 1813-1814*. Boston: Little, Brown and Company, 1981.

Collins, William R. *Ohio : The Buckeye State*. Englewood Cliffs, New Jersey: Prentice-Hall, 1968.

Hartzell, Lawrence W. *Ohio Moravian Music*. Winston-Salem, North Carolina: Moravian Music Foundation Press, 1988.

Hatcher, Harlan. *The Buckeye Country: A Pageant of Ohio*. New York : G. P. Putnam's Sons, 1947.

Havighurst, Walter. *Ohio : A Bicentennial History*. New York: W. W. Norton and Company, 1976.

Howe, Henry. *Historical Collections of Ohio*. Cincinnati: C. J. Krehbiel and Company, 1908.

Hulbert, Archer Butler. *The Ohio River : A Course of Empire*. New York : G. P. Putnam's Sons, 1906.

Hunter, Louis C. *Steamboats on the Western Rivers: An Economic and Technological History*. Cambridge, Massachusetts: Harvard University Press, 1949.

Knepper, George W. *Ohio and Its People*. Kent, Ohio: Kent State University Press, 1989.

Knepper, George W. *An Ohio Portrait*. Columbus: Ohio American Revolution Bicentennial Advisory Commission, 1976.

MacLean, J. P. *Shakers of Ohio*. Columbus: F. J. Heer Printing Company, 1907.

Osburn, Mary Hubbell. *Ohio Composers and Musical Authors*. Columbus: F. J. Heer Printing Company, 1942.

Overman, William. *Ohio Town Names*. Akron: Atlantic Press, 1959.

Perry, Dick. *Ohio : A Personal Portrait of the Seventeenth State*. Garden City, New York: Doubleday and Company, 1969.

Ramage, James A. *Rebel Raider : The Life of General John Hunt Morgan*. Lexington, Kentucky: University Press of Kentucky, 1986.

Randall, Emilius O. and Ryan, Daniel J. *History of Ohio : The Rise and Progress of an American State*. New York : The Century History Company, 1912.

Roseboom, Eugene H. and Weisenburger, Francis P. *A History of Ohio*. 2nd ed. Columbus: Ohio Historical Society, 1984.

Ryan, Daniel J. *A History of Ohio*. Columbus : A. H. Smythe, 1888.

Shoemaker, Dacia Custer. *Choose You This Day: The Legacy of the Hanbys*. Westerville, Ohio: Westerville Historical Society, 1983.

Siebert, Wilbur Henry. *The Mysteries of Ohio's Underground Railroad*. Columbus: Long's College Book Company, 1951.

Siebert, Wilbur Henry. *The Underground Railroad From Slavery to Freedom*. Gloucester, Massachusetts: Peter Smith, 1968.

Smith, Thomas H., ed. *An Ohio Reader: 1750 to the Civil War*. Grand Rapids, Michigan: William B. Eerdmans Publishing Company, 1975.

Sprigg, June and Larkin, David. *Shaker Life, Work, and Art*. New York: Stewart, Tabori, and Chang, 1987

Stille, Samuel Harden. *Ohio Builds a Nation*. 4th ed. Chicago: Arlendale Book House, 1953.

Street, James. *The Struggle for Tennessee: Tupelo to Stones River*. Alexandria, Virginia: Time-Life Books, 1985.

Trevorrow, Frank W. *Ohio's Canals: History, Description, Biography*. Oberlin, Ohio: Frank W. Trevorrow, 1973.

Wilcox, Frank. *The Ohio Canals*. Kent: Kent State University Press, 1969.

Winkler, Suzanne. *The Smithsonian Guide to Historic America: The Great Lakes States*. New York: Stewart, Tabori, and Chang, 1989.

Song Source Bibliography

Carmer, Carl, ed., *Songs of the Rivers of America*. New York: Farrar & Rinehart, 1942.

Densmore, Frances. *Chippewa Music*. Washington, D.C.: Bureau of American Ethnology, Smithsonian Institution, 1910.

Dolph, Edward Arthur. *Sound Off! Soldier Songs from Yankee Doodle to Parley Voo*. New York: Cosmopolitan Book Corporation, 1929.

Eddy, Mary O., comp. *Ballads and Songs From Ohio*. New York: J. J. Augustin Publishers, 1939.

Fowke, Edith and Mills, Alan. *Canada's Story in Song*. Toronto: W. J. Gage, n.d.

Fowke, Edith Fulton and Johnston, Richard. *Folk Songs of Canada*. Waterloo, Ontario: Waterloo Music Company, 1954.

Fowke, Edith Fulton and Johnston, Richard. *Folk Songs of Quebec*. Waterloo, Ontario: Waterloo Music Company, 1957.

Glass, Paul and Singer, Louis C., eds. *Songs of Forest and River Folk*. New York: Grosset & Dunlap Publishers, 1967.

Hullfish, William. *The Canaller's Songbook*. York, Pennsylvania: The American Canal and Transportation Center, 1984.

Jordan, Philip P. and Kessler, Lillian. *Songs of Yesterday : A Song Anthology of American Life*. Garden City, New York: Doubleday, Doran and Company, 1941.

Lomax, John A. and Lomax, Alan, comps. *American Ballads and Folk Songs*. New York: The Macmillan Company, 1934.

Neeser, Robert W. *American Naval Songs and Ballads*. New Haven, Connecticut: Yale University Press, 1938.

Nye, Pearl R., Papers. Columbus: Ohio Historical Society, MSS 60 ; MSS 826.

O'Flynn, Ann C. and Carriere, Joseph Medard, comps. *Folk Songs of Old Vincennes*. Chicago: H. T. Fitzsimons Company, 1946.

Papale, Henry, comp. *Banners, Buttons, and Songs : A Pictorial Review and Capsule Almanac of America's Presidential Campaigns*. Cincinnati : World Library Publications, 1968.

Rickaby, Francis, ed. *Ballads and Songs of the Shanty-Boy*. Cambridge, Massachusetts : Harvard University Press, 1926.

Silber, Irwin, comp. *Songs America Voted By*. Harrisburg, Pennsylvania : Stackpole Books, 1971.

Silber, Irwin, comp. *Songs of the Civil War*. New York: Columbia University Press, 1960.

Thomas, Cloea, ed. *Scenes and Songs of the Ohio-Erie Canal*. Columbus: Ohio Historical Society, 1971.

Thomas, Jean and Leeder, Joseph A. *The Singin' Gatherin'*. New York: Silver Burdett Company, 1939.

Thompson, Harold W., ed. *A Pioneer Songster : Texts From the Stevens-Douglass Manuscript of Western New York, 1841-1856*. Ithaca, New York : Cornell University Press, 1958.

Ward, William R. *The American Bicentennial Songbook.* New York : Charles Hansen Educational Music and Books, 1975.

Wenner, Hilda E. and Freilicher, Elizabeth. *Here's To the Women : 100 Songs For and About American Women.* Syracuse, New York : Syracuse University Press, 1987.

Discography

Buckley, Bruce. *Ohio Valley Ballads*. Folkways Records (FP 23-2).

Gibson, Bob. *Folksongs of Ohio*. Stinson Records (SLP 76).

Grimes, Anne. *Ohio State Ballads*. Folkways Records (FH 5217).

Houk, Gloria Martin. *Songs of the Ohio Country*. Mark Records.

House, Wallace. *Ballads of the War of 1812: 1791-1814*. Folkways Records (FA 2163).

House, Wallace. *Ballads of the War of 1812: 1814-1836*. Folkways Records (FA 2164).

About the Author

Elizabeth Anne Salt is a librarian at Otterbein College is Westerville, Ohio. She plays several folk instruments, including the mountain dulcimer, bowed psaltery, and autoharp. She has been performing both with folk music groups and as a solo player for eight years. Her musical interests include traditional historical ballads, old-time religious songs, and folk tunes from the British Isles.

To order additional copies of this book, or other books published by Enthea Press, please call us toll free: 1-800-336-7769. We will be happy to charge orders against MasterCard, VISA, or American Express—or answer your questions. Please call between 8 and 6 Monday through Thursday, holidays excepted.

Enthea Press
14230 Phillips Circle
Alpharetta, GA 30201